Conversations with a Poet

Inviting Poetry into K-12 Classrooms

Betsy Franco

Richard C. Owen Publishers, Inc.
Katonah, New York

Grateful acknowledgment is made to the following for permission to reprint previously published material:

"Painting a Summer Day" by Kris Aro McKleod first appeared in *Whatever the Weather,* Scholastic, Inc, 2001. © 2001 by Kris Aro McKleod. Used by permission of author.

"New Honesty" by Jessie Childress first appeared in *Things I Have to Tell You, poems and writing by teenage girls,* Candlewick Press, 2001. © 2001 by Jessie Childress. Used by permission of author.

"He Shaved His Head," by Rene Ruiz first appeared in *You Hear Me? poems and writing by teenage boys,* Candlewick Press, 2000. © 2000 by Rene Ruiz. Every effort has been made to contact the author for permission to reprint this poem. We regret any oversights that may have occurred and would be happy to rectify them in future printings of this work.

Library of Congress Cataloging-in-Publication Data

Franco, Betsy.
  Conversations with a poet : inviting poetry into K-12 classrooms / by Betsy Franco.
     p. cm.
Summary: "Presents ideas for teaching forms, elements, and writing of poetry kindergarten to high school and describes and provides teachers with samples and bibliographies for sixteen poetic forms"--Provided by publisher.
Includes bibliographical references and index.
  ISBN-13: 978-1-57274-740-1
  ISBN-10: 1-57274-740-4
  1. Poetry--Study and teaching (Elementary) 2. Poetry--Study and teaching (Secondary) 3. Creative writing (Elementary education) 4. Creative writing (Secondary education) I. Title.
  LB1576.F677 2005
  808.1'071--dc22
                              2005027135
                                 CIP

Richard C. Owen Publishers, Inc.
PO Box 585
Katonah, NY 10536
914-232-3903; fax 914-232-3977
www.RCOwen.com

Acquisitions Editor: Darcy H. Bradley
Production Manager: Phyllis Morrison
Cover Design: Kell Miller-Arrow

Printed in the United States of America

9   8   7   6   5   4   3   2   1

For Maria Damon who has taught me everything important I know about poetry . . . especially how to keep an open mind about it.

TABLE OF CONTENTS

SECTION I

RATIONALES & PRACTICAL IDEAS FOR TEACHING POETRY

SECTION II

UNPACKING THE POETRY FORMS

PREFACE

When I was a teacher and when I started writing poems, a poet's explanation of the basics of poetry would have been very helpful. In the following chapters, I share what I've learned about reading, writing, and teaching poetry because I have found that knowledge is power.

As a practicing poet, I am letting you in on the secrets that have taken me time to understand and that I know only from writing poems, day in and day out, and from discussing poetry with fellow poets. I invite you to view poetry from a unique vantage point, from inside the mind of a poet who loves poetry.

ACKNOWLEDGMENTS

Thank you to all my poet friends who inspire me and who contributed their thoughts and feelings about poetry to the book. I am grateful to my critique group for giving me invaluable feedback on my poetry, and to my editor Darcy Bradley who encouraged me to dig deeper at every stage of the book.

INTRODUCTION

I have been writing poetry, in collections and in picture books, for twenty-five years, and I have been publishing poetry written by teenagers since the year 2000. I feel that every year my own poetry improves. One of the reasons it improves is that I write every day. Another is that I read many other poets. I also learn from a friend and professor of English, Maria Damon, who teaches me about poetry when she reacts to the poems I write and when we write books together. To further strengthen my writing, I get feedback from my writing group of fellow children's-book writers who meet with me every month, and I take classes in poetry at a nearby university as often as possible.

I wrote this guidebook to help you in your teaching of poetry and to support your students' poetry writing and your own. My intent is to show how to adapt the creative processes of practicing poets to the classroom setting and to add to your knowledge of poetry and the poetry forms. My hope is that it will encourage you to teach poetry all year long, instead of saving it for April, National Poetry Month.

HOW THIS BOOK IS ORGANIZED

The book is divided into two sections. Section I is a frank discussion of writing and teaching poetry from a poet's point of view. It gives you inside information that is not always included in educational books. This section provides a philosophical foundation and a practical set of ideas for teaching poetry. Section II specifically targets sixteen different poetry forms. In each chapter, I unpack a form and provide sample poems and bibliographical citations as models.

Section I begins with a rationale for teaching poetry and for teaching the poetry forms, in particular, to bolster your resolve to teach poetry throughout the year. I've also enumerated my reasons for choosing the poetry forms included in the book. The next chapters in Section I explain the nuts and bolts—the elements of poetry and how to read and discuss poetry with students. The last chapters of this section are intended to help you and your students through the exciting process of teaching and writing in the poetry forms. These chapters include practical suggestions and support for teacher demonstrations and ideas for jump-starting creativity. They also present a model for "revision as experimentation" and give a variety of suggestions for publishing and presenting student poetry.

Throughout Section I, I have included the voices of my poet friends, ranging from outstanding poets who are recent college graduates to renowned children's poets. My purpose is for you to see that everyone has a different process, as your students will, and to let you in on the inner thoughts of practicing poets. I also provided biographies of these poets at the back of the book so that students would understand that there is no stereotypical poet—that they, too, can be poets, regardless of their interests or personalities.

Section II thoroughly explains the poetry forms, which are in alphabetical order. Every chapter includes historical background, characteristics of the form, and "What This Form Offers." This latter portion specifies the benefits of teaching each form and shows how to meet objectives of current standards. To make a link to children's lives, I've listed everyday parallels of the poetry forms as well. The chart on page 52 provides a list of the forms from most accessible to most complicated. The first page of every poetry form also indicates suggested grade levels.

After the first informational pages in Section II, you will find sample poems at your fingertips. These samples include a primary poem for grades K-2, an intermediate poem for grades 3-5, and a middle school/high school poem for grades 6-12, when appropriate. For example, the samples for the sonnet are only for grades 9-12. However, when you read my poems, you will see that many more of the poetry forms are appropriate for elementary school children than you might expect. Having had teaching experience in grades K-12, in some capacity, and by visiting classrooms every day, I have been able to keep each age group in my mind's eye while writing the poems in this book.

For each poetry form, I included a writing demonstration (what I call a "think-through") that reveals my thinking as I wrote one of the sample poems.

Bibliographies of books and Internet sites where additional sample poems can be found are located at the end of each form. While compiling these extensive bibliographies, my purpose was to provide a varied body of poetry—classical, diverse, fun, serious. I also made an effort to cite a wide range of poems, from easily accessible poems to avant-garde poetry, that will push the envelope for your students.

HOW TO USE THIS BOOK

Conversations with a Poet can be used in a variety of ways. Depending on your comfort level with poetry, you can pick and choose from the chapters in Section I, which are meant to provide inspiration, background, and practical suggestions for teaching the poetry forms.

In Section II, the poetry forms are arranged in alphabetical order, but a chart on page 52 lists them from most accessible to most complicated. One very workable option is to teach them in order of accessibility, teaching one approximately every two weeks. Of course, you might feel more comfortable starting with the forms you are familiar with and moving on to the new ones. Or you could stimulate your students by starting with forms that neither of you has ever explored. These might include visual poems, found poems, and sestinas.

Another approach is to tie the forms to the curriculum. For example, students could write ballads or persona poems that relate to American history. Blues poems could fit into a study of the Civil War, slavery, or civil rights. Students could write free verse or cinquains about the poetic aspects of scientific subjects such as metamorphosis or cloud formations. You could use the beats and the syllables in limericks and haiku, or the patterns in a sestina, as part of a math lesson. If conflicts arise in the classroom, you could use multi-voice poems to brainstorm solutions. Free verse could be an ongoing part of daily journaling.

Although this text implies that students will be writing their own poetry for all forms, you might only study the structure and the sample poems for some of the forms. For others, student writing may be the main event. For instance, intermediate students might appreciate the sestina about the dog at the beach, but they probably wouldn't write one of their own. Similarly, kindergartners enjoy limericks, and some of the samples are meant for them, but they probably won't write any of their own. On the other hand, some of the forms that might be out of reach for individuals can be fun to write cooperatively as a class. Kindergartners might write a list poem together about what they like to do with their friends. Intermediate students could write a renga as a class.

In general, the informational pages for each form in Section II can be your back-up when introducing each poetry form to students. The sample poems form a handy mini-anthology of model poems to jump-start student writing. The bibliographies are meant to expand on my sample poems because I have a particular style, and students need to be exposed to a wide variety of diverse poetry and poets.

There are several ways in which Sections I and II can be used in tandem. Specific pages in Section I will be helpful when students are in the workshopping stages or the revision/experimentation stages. (See pages 37-38 for possible ways of workshopping a poem, and pages 34-36 for ideas on revising.) If you want to teach specific elements of poetry writing such as line breaks, you can use Chapter 3 in Section I for backup. Finally, when it comes to publishing or presenting student poems, you can refer back to Chapter 9.

Another way to use Sections I and II together relates to the poets quoted throughout Section I. I purposely included these poets in the bibliographies, and their biographies are in alphabetical order at the back of the book. The quotes, poems, and biographies can be used together to study a particular poet's unique style. For easy access, the index includes each poet's name.

RESOURCES IN THIS BOOK

I've been a classroom teacher, so I know how little time teachers have. Now that I'm a writer, I have time to write the books I wish I'd had as a teacher. In this book I offer some time-saving ideas.

Demonstrations

In Section II, I call my demonstrations "Think-throughs." There are 16 demonstrations at your fingertips that can be used with your students and that can serve as models for your own demonstrations. I showed my thinking and strategies as I wrote one of the sample poems for each poetry form. These demonstrations show how I revise, or what I call "experiment," from first draft to last. In addition, I wrote brief notes for each sample poem, pointing out such things as poetic elements and strategies I used.

Teaching Schedules

On pages 48-49, you will find three different scheduling possibilities that show how to include poetry when you are planning your instructional week.

Poetry Forms Chart

The chart on page 52 shows the forms in what I see as a teachable order, beginning with the list poem, the form I consider easiest, and ending with the sestina, a more challenging form. The chart also shows which forms I recommend for different grade levels. Obviously, you can pick and choose and rearrange.

Bibliographies

With diversty in mind, I researched and included an extensive bibliography that appears at the end of each poetry form in Section II. A number of citations are online because the Internet is a very accessible source of poetry. Any poem or author mentioned in the text is included in the bibliography. Page references are cited in the chapters to make it easier for you to find the bibliographic information.

Student Handouts

I wrote all the chapters in Section I in such a way that they could be shared with students verbatim. Particularly, the charts and questions in Chapter 7 on revision/experimentation, the read-throughs on pages 18-22, and the workshopping questions in chapter 7 can be handed to students at appropriate grade levels. In Section II, the sample poems for each poetry form, available at different grade levels, can be photocopied for student use, along with the "think-through" for each of the 16 poetry forms.

Poet Biographies

All the poets who are quoted in this book or whose poetry is reproduced in this book are part of the "Poet Biographies" section. I elicited these quotes from a diverse group of poets.

Glossary

The glossary is annotated with examples to clarify some of the terms used in the book. Throughout the text I refer you to the glossary for further detail.

Poetry and Standards

Many teachers worry that there isn't enough time in the day to teach poetry. In Section II, for every poetry form I included a section called "What This Form Offers," in which I listed the benefits of each form, as they relate to learning standards. You might be surprised to find out how many of the standards can be met through poetry writing, besides the ones you would expect, such as introducing conventional poetry forms and understanding terms such as *metaphor* and *simile*. For example, the acrostic and sestina offer opportunities for logical thinking. The sonnet is about presenting a hypothesis and coming to conclusions. The list poem encourages students to think about sequencing. The diamanté provides an opportunity to emphasize parts of speech. Students will be writing persuasively and descriptively in odes. In general, students will be interpreting and synthesizing the meaning of poems, comparing and contrasting different forms of poetry, and practicing fluency by reading poems aloud, particularly their own. They will be learning the stages of the writing process, from brainstorming to a final draft, and reading notable literary selections. Many curricular tie-ins—ways to use poetry to enrich the basic curriculum—exist. A number of these curricular ideas are listed on page xi.

AN INVITATION

It's time to start. Pull up a chair and let's talk about poetry in a different way— the way poets do. I'll show you an approach to poetry that will make teaching, reading, and writing poems a fun, inspiring, and relevant part of your day and your students' day, while meeting the requirements of learning standards at the same time. This approach is one that will impact lives, that will encourage your students to discover who they are as individuals, and will encourage them to "tell their stories." This approach will invite you to do the same.

SECTION I

RATIONALES AND PRACTICAL IDEAS FOR TEACHING POETRY

1   WHY TEACH POETRY?

If I couldn't write poetry, I would not be a happy person. If my pencil and paper were taken away, I would write on the sidewalk with stones or on the beach with sticks. I need to describe my world and what I find important in it through poetry in order to feel comfortable in my skin.

> "There is nothing like poetry in the whole wide world. Eat it, drink it, sleep with it. Make it a part of your everyday life. Make poetry YOURS."
> —*Lee Bennett Hopkins**

> "It helps increase my creativity—it's sort of like a brain exercise. It can help me calm down 'cause I have something else to focus on, not my sadness or my angriness."
> —*Robin Anwyl, age 8*

> "I like that way of describing things [writing poetry]. Sometimes I just sit for an hour and nothing happens. Sometimes everything just comes at one time . . . It relaxes me."
> —*Laura Rose, age 11*

> "If I don't know anything else about myself, I know I can write."
> —*High school poet from Detroit*

TELLING OUR STORIES

I can't be the only person in the world who has an intense need to write. I know I'm not alone when I talk to other poets, writers, and artists who express something similar. But even if every student in your class doesn't have the same need as I do, every student does have a need to tell his or her story in some form: writing, art, music, dance, creative writing, computer programming, fancy skateboarding, or some other form of creativity.

Because the arts are being lost to the focus on learning standards in many schools, it is so important to teach poetry—and not just in April, National Poetry Month. In fact, the beginning of the year is an excellent place to start. Of all the ways students have to express themselves, poetry writing is one of the most powerful ways for them to tell their stories inside the classroom walls.

I hear teachers saying there's not enough time for poetry, but the irony of that

*Biographies of all quoted poets are found on pages 209-212.

statement is two-fold. First, poetry meets many of the current learning standards. Second, if students are given time to write their stories and tell who they are, they will be more open to other areas of the curriculum. For some students, nothing else can take place until they have told their story.

Think about it on a personal level. Once you've been heard on an issue that is a concern for you, once a friend has been willing to listen to your story, aren't you more open to risk, to learn, to interact, to try new things, or to learn new subjects you didn't even think you'd be interested in?

EFFECTS OF STORYTELLING

In 2000, I compiled a book called *You Hear Me? poems and writing by teenage boys*. One mother said her son stopped considering suicide once he wrote and published his story in this book. Another boy stayed in high school. Another poet from the heart of Detroit wrote a poem entitled "I Never Told This to Anyone;" the title speaks for itself. Other teachers and parents have told me that teenagers had turned around from very dark places after reading poems in the book that they could relate to, poems that told their story. Why wait until adolescence? Or if students are adolescents, why not start now? Now is a great time to listen and to allow the storytelling—through poetry in the classroom.

> "Like any kind of artistic expression, part of it [writing poetry] is catharsis, it's a release. I also write because I feel that I speak for the underrepresented. It's performance poetry I do, you know . . . It's social commentary."
> —*Mahogany Foster*

> "I write poetry because it helps me see patterns and find order in my thoughts and observations. Often, I'll have a concern or obsession that only becomes apparent to me after I've unwittingly written about it several times."
> —*Brian Laidlaw*

> "I write because I need to. On days when I don't write I feel that things are more grey. It simply brightens my days, so I try to write first thing in the morning . . ."
> —*Renato Rosaldo*

ADVANTAGES OF POETRY

Poetry has an advantage as a channel for storytelling—it is short. My ideas come in short spurts, which is perfect for poetry. Many students share this economic way of thinking. And most students have the ability to focus for a short time—enough time to write a poem. If students' first attempts at poetry are accepted without harsh judgment by their teachers, they gain the confidence to build on from there.

Poetry can be about anything. This concept can help the reluctant writer. In one third grade class, a boy rubbed his head and told me he wasn't "good at this." I told him that was okay, but he should know that he could write about anything.

Anything goes. He was wearing a baseball cap, so I mentioned sports. But by the end of the session, he had written a short, dramatic poem about a raccoon with rabies. After I read it, I looked up at him, and he had an unabashed smile on his face.

Poetry is powerful enough to hold strong feelings. Stephen Healey teaches creative writing in a maximum security prison. Below he has summarized the role of poetry in the life of Daryl, one of the young men in his class.

> "Faced with control, intimidation, or deprivation from the corrections system and from other convicts, only two options seem available to Daryl: be passive and let yourself be diminished, or be destructive and let yourself explode . . . creativity, however, gives a prisoner a way to express that paradox, to release it, to discover and rediscover its productivity."
> —Stephen Healey

Poetry can range from silly to deeply serious in tone. All students in your class, from the outgoing student with an irrepressible sense of humor to the one who is quiet and self-reflective, can feel comfortable with poetry. Some poems are very intense. Some poems are just about a poet having fun with the English language and playing with words.

> "I'm playing in the vast sandbox of the English language . . ."
> —Paul Fleischman

> "For me, wordplay is the pinnacle. Verbal contortions, surprising juxtapositions, great puns . . . it's very much like going after the brass ring, the rosetta stone."
> —J. Patrick Lewis

> "I've always liked the sound of words, enough that I like to mix them up and make up new words. I didn't realize how much I did that until the spell checker went down the page saying 'This isn't right, this isn't right.' I'd made up eight or nine words."
> —Sarah Wilson

Poetry is ultimately a way to get back to the time in kindergarten when everyone wanted to tell her or his story. No matter what was going on, someone might raise a hand and start telling about what happened that morning before school. Poetry can open that door again.

> "Poetry is important to teach in schools because kids need permission, the time, and the opportunity to pay attention to the world, to explore their feelings as they grapple with the issue of just how they fit into that world. Poetry gives kids a chance to fool around with language. Poetry gives kids a chance to be a musician with words."
> —Paul Janeczko

BUILDING A COMMUNITY OF POETS

I've noticed that something magical happens when a group of students is writing poetry. The energy in the room is palpable. If one student shares her work, it gives energy to other students. Students raise the bar for each other about how experimental they can be, about how honest they can be, about how much fun they can have writing poetry, about how present they can be while writing.

> "To be in a roomful of writers collectively engaged in the same basic task, yet fully in our own composing process is a remarkable experience."
> — *Stephen Healey*

For this reason, I like to use time in class to write with students of all ages, from kindergarten through twelfth grade. And I like to write along with everyone else, so I'm part of the community.

Of course, building a community of poets also takes place by building an atmosphere of trust. The classroom can be an environment based on positive feedback and helpful questions, where there are no mistakes, where uniqueness is valued, where students feel comfortable reading aloud. This sense of community can be strengthened further by having poetry readings and/or open mic sessions, where everyone supports everyone else, where everyone takes risks.

When I go into a classroom as a visiting poet, I have a very short time to build a community, but it's one of my main goals. From the beginning, I try to show the students that I respect their ideas and their creativity by honoring their questions and any suggestions they make in our brainstorming sessions. I try to show that I respect them as individuals by delighting in their unusual responses and their unique senses of humor. It's not hard for me to show that I love students, because I do. I show them that I trust them by demonstrating my writing process or by reading one of my poems in progress and revising it in front of them. I give them constructive feedback by pointing out lines of their poetry that are strong and creative. I apologize if I step over their boundaries; for example, one girl wanted me to read her poem to myself, not in a whisper by her side. In one class where we felt like a community, the students suggested spontaneously that we share our poems. After each volunteer shared, the students broke into applause. One boy, who the teacher said lacked confidence, was the first to read his "Ode to Beagle Puppies."

Poetry can be healing, it can be magic, it can stir up creative energy, and it can build community in the classroom.

2 HOW IS POETRY DIFFERENT FROM OTHER FORMS OF WRITING?

> "I love poetry, love the compression, the word play, the way thoughts bump up against one another."
> —*Jane Yolen*

> "I think that I probably write poetry more often than I write prose because from the time I was a young child I've always loved rhythmic music, particularly jazz, and the rhyming lyrics of songs."
> —*Bobbi Katz*

When writing an essay, you think about an introductory paragraph, topic sentences, and a conclusion. When you write a persuasive paper, you try to sell your viewpoint, and you need to make clear, cohesive points. Other forms of writing have their key elements as well.

When writing poetry, one difference is that a poem is often shorter, more succinct, more economical than other forms of writing. The line breaks are a key element of poetry. But one of the most beautiful aspects of writing poetry is the freedom of it.

> "Poetry comes from the heart or lower. Essay writing comes more from the head or the throat. If I'm lucky, a poem goes straight to what matters most . . ."
> —*Renato Rosaldo*

POETRY AS FREEDOM

> "I write poetry because I am a rebel, a pioneer, who hates to be bound by formulas, rules, and guidelines. In poetry I can be as free as a bird."
> —*Thomas Yeahpau*

I remember when one of my sons first took photography in high school, he was trying to do it "right." When I suggested that he take pictures of whatever was meaningful to him, that he should photograph the world the way he saw it, his shoulders literally relaxed and he smiled. He immediately started taking pictures of subjects I never could have predicted he would choose. His photos were intriguing and revealed something important about him, to himself. That's what I think art is about—self-discovery.

Poetry needs to be this way even when poetry forms are introduced as guides for writing. Poetry forms can be stimulating and interesting, but they don't always need to be followed precisely. Granted, some students will feel more comfortable and safer with a strict form. Others will rebel against the form. It doesn't matter. Underneath it all, poetry is about surprise, a new point of view, an insight, an emotion, an unusual vantage point, a telling detail, something the poet has noticed with his or her own eyes, a new way to use language. So, following the form exactly or rebelling against it reveals something about the poet.

> "I motivate my students to be as creative as they can, and I tell them to value their identities, to take pride. They are challenged to be original, to be silly, to be unpredictable, to be curious, and not only to ask questions, but to answer them by channeling into that raw space within themselves."
> —Stephan Johnson

Imagine walking in nature with someone, stepping into their body, and seeing a scene through their eyes. Every person in the room, including you, perceives interactions, surroundings, memories, coming events, and feelings differently. One gift of poetry is that you get a glimpse into a student's viewpoint, insides, or unique stance.

FORM AS SPRINGBOARD

Poetry forms can be jumping-off points. They help when a student is faced with a white sheet of paper. They help turn that blank page into a beautiful white piece of paper, ripe with potential for telling a story that needs to be told. They give a structure for telling that story. They give a starting point, a way to get into the story.

Poetry forms also offer ways for students to get to places where they've never been. When I try a new form, I find feelings and places in my mind and imagination that I've never tapped. Different students will respond to different forms differently. A student with a mathematical or logical mind may enjoy the more rule-governed limerick, haiku, or sestina, whereas free verse may appeal to a free-spirited student.

> "Creative writing classes, so I'm told (never having had one), insist that you find your own voice. I suppose that's a reasonable objective, but mine is to write in a hundred voices, and thus to mine as many forms as possible."
> —J. Patrick Lewis

> "Sometimes my poems go through many, many forms—from structured to free verse to prose poem then into a three line poem then back to free verse again!"
> —Miriam Stone

> "Limitations are almost always helpful. Working in form forces you to streamline your ideas and images and often results in a stronger poem."
> —Brian Laidlaw

Since poetry is about freedom of expression, it's most important during poetry time, versus other writing time, to let students know that it's a time when they won't be judged. The atmosphere you set is very important. And you need to also remember not to judge yourself during that time. Experiment with not judging anything during poetry time.

> "Forms are suggestions. Many of the greatest poets made their marks by changing the forms to fit their needs. When in doubt, err on the side of being open."
> —Maria Damon

THE OTHER SIDE OF THE COIN

For some students, poetry is their joy. For some, reading and writing are tedious, hard work. But you can build even on negative feelings that some students harbor. A substitute teacher told me she had trouble with a few students when an assignment was to write about being thankful, about things they liked. I suggested that the resisters could have written about what they didn't like. Some students need to express "the other side of the coin" no matter what the coin is, because that's what their insides are about at the moment. Once they get those ideas out, and they're not judged, they may actually be able to get to something positive. Poetry allows for that.

Some students think poetry is about subjects that hold no interest for them. But poetry can be about anything. A list poem (see Chapter 20), for example, can engage students to write about feelings, their pets, building robots, sports, war, hiking in nature, divorce, their video games, something they're sad about, siblings, recess, their skateboards, black holes, their gardens, their favorite stuffed animals, depression, friends. Poetry makes room for whatever is inside.

> "Poetry is an answer to the questions that life throws my way, a chance to converse with myself, a chance to yell back, a chance to highlight something motivational and beautiful. Writing poetry is a response, a science, an action as sure as breathing."
> —Stephan Johnson

PUSHING THE ENVELOPE

The important thing to remember is that the poetry forms are not set in stone. Even haiku, with its 5 syllables, 7 syllables, 5 syllables form, is disputed among poets because the syllables in the Japanese language are very short sounds. Some poets say that 5, 7, 5 is too many syllables. As a result, many poets write haiku without counting the syllables. There's room to stretch the envelope with any form.

Throughout this book, I've written sample poems that follow the "rules" because they are common starting points. For me, learning new forms and trying to follow them opened me up to many new poets and poems and gave me access to new forms when writing my own poetry collections. It can do this for the students as well. But the rules are often broken in modern and post-modern poetry. If it is in a student's nature to break rules, let them. The form will still have served to get her or him to a different place of exploration.

That's what poetry is. It's exploration. Let students excavate and explore freely. No helmets, no rules.

> "Poetry is not imprisoned just to one place or culture. It can be the political rant and rave by literary revolutionaries, or the rearrangement of words found on the back of a cereal box. Poetry is easily accessible to the public and gives voice to anyone with an imaginative mind."
> — *Stephan Johnson*

3 UNDERSTANDING RHYME, LINE BREAKS, AND OTHER SELECTED ELEMENTS OF POETRY

Many aspects of poetry are misunderstood but are not always addressed. The study of the elements of poetry is vast; however, poets often think about and notice certain basic concepts in the poems they read and write.

RHYME

Rhyme is a common aspect of children's poetry. It's fun for children to read, especially young children, but it is deceptively complex to write. Actually, it takes a great deal of skill and just the right touch to write a rhyming poem that is effective.

Rhyme is often forced when students attempt to write it. They are writing about a specific subject and they know what they want to say, but they can't find the appropriate rhyming word. They usually end up forcing the rhyme by creating convoluted sentences or phrases or by using words that have nothing to do with the context of their poems. Sometimes students let the rhyme create the poem, using simple rhymes, such as *red* and *bed* or *sun* and *fun,* that don't really say anything. If young poets say what they mean in the first place, without trying to rhyme, their poems are usually much more powerful and have a music and rhythm of their own. A third grader said it beautifully:

> "It has a tune but not rhyming."
> —*Young-Ju Lee*

When students are using rhyme for forms that traditionally rhyme, such as limericks, ballads, and blues poems, the results are generally not as forced. The ballad has a natural rhythm to it, which helps with the rhyme. The limerick, with its sing-songy, familiar rhythm and rhyme, presents an opportunity for students to think about rhyme as a puzzle. The rhyme in a blues poem is often a slant rhyme, involving words that almost rhyme, such as *messy* and *sassy.* This type of rhyme is usually more natural-sounding.

> "Lots of things come to me in rhyme—I think that way. One of the best ways to rhyme is using a rhyming dictionary. Or you can rearrange the words in sentences so the rhyme is at the end. The best way to write interesting rhymes is to have a good vocabulary."
> —*Joy Hulme*

As anyone can see from reading Regie Routman's *Kids' Poems* series, when children are freed from rhyme, the results are stunning and moving. Even when I rhyme in a sample poem, I recommend that students do not rhyme in their poems, except in the forms that require it.

However, one form of rhyme that students might have fun noticing and using in poems is called *internal rhyme*. In this type of rhyme, a rhyming word appears in the middle of a verse, or stanza, rather than at the end. Technically, the rhyming words can be scattered anywhere in the poem, even at the end of a line, as long as two or more words that rhyme do not appear at the ends of lines. Internal rhyme can be exciting when you notice or use it:

> The <u>clack</u> of my skateboard
> as my <u>pack</u> bounces on
> my <u>back</u>—that's the beat
> on the way to school.

PUNCTUATION

As for capitalization and punctuation, there are many misconceptions. Poets often punctuate a poem similarly to prose. If you read the poem like a paragraph, you capitalize the beginnings of sentences and place commas and periods where they naturally fall. If the poem is a series of phrases, they are often separated by commas with a period at the end of the thought. Some poets leave off all punctuation and capitalization, even making *I* into *i*. Sometimes commas are left off because a line break signals a pause, and a comma isn't necessary. In the poem below, there could have been a comma after *speak,* but it's not necessary.

> Monsters under
> my bed
> never speak
> never move
> but they are
> there.

In the classic poems of the past, the first word in each line is capitalized. But in modern poetry, this is out of vogue. Nowadays, when a poet starts each line with a capital, the poet is usually trying to create an effect, such as formality, strength, or emphasis. The capitals in this new version of the poem make it scarier.

> Monsters under
> My bed
> Never speak
> Never move
> But they are
> There.

LINE BREAKS

Line breaks is a critical topic because it is one of the distinguishing features of most poems.

Some poems have a natural rhythm, almost like a song. It's easy to know where to break the line.

> The school is closed and dark,
>
> and the teachers are at home.
>
> The kids are all asleep,
>
> but I'm writing this little poem.

Sometimes the line breaks where the thought ends, or where the reader or the poet naturally pauses.

> When summer is departing
>
> and fall is arriving,
>
> the wind whips through the trees
>
> and spooks the cat.

Some poets break the line according to syllables, using the same number of syllables in each line. The number of syllables might vary from line to line, but each stanza or verse has the same pattern.

The cats raced across	(5 syllables)
the office.	(3 syllables)
They made the papers	(5 syllables)
fly like birds.	(3 syllables)

Sometimes the line breaks are in unexpected places. By breaking a line in the middle of a thought, the poet teases you into going on to the next line with anticipation. A thought can even go from one verse, or stanza, to another. This is called *enjambment* or *run-on*.

> Home is where you
>
> can shrug off your
>
> backpack and your
>
> worries, sling around
>
> your complaints about
>
> impossible questions on the science
>
> test, and supposedly
>
> best . . .

Some poets, such as e.e. cummings, broke lines in a playful way, often in the middle of words. (See Bibliography, Visual Poetry, page 207.)

Poets often spend time experimenting with placing the line break in different places to see how it affects the way the poem reads, its meaning, and its appearance.

WHITE SPACE

What about white space in poems? Except for the prose poem that is written in paragraph form, most poetry has more white space than other forms of writing. The lines are usually short enough that white space appears to the right or left of the poem, or both, if the poem is in the center of the page.

Poems are conventionally left-justified, but actually the text can be anywhere on the page. Some poets play with spacing. In a poem about rain, the words might be separated and placed all over the page, like the raindrops in a storm. The words can look like what they're saying.

> rain
>
>   drip-
>
>   ped
>
>   and
>
> drop-
>
>   ped
>
>   down
>
>   my
>
>   neck

Indentations are a way to play with white space. In a poem about a walk, the poet might indent as she's going around a bend, for example.

> I tiptoed down the path
>
>   and around the bend
>
> to find my sister hiding
>
>   under
>
> the willow tree

An indentation can signal opposites or two voices speaking.

> I looked inside
>
>   and outside
>
> but she was nowhere.

Indenting can place emphasis on a part of a poem.

My shadow copied me as I

> hopped

> skipped

> and boogied.

WORD CHOICE AND PACING

Poets can manipulate the pace, or how quickly you read a poem. Some words are sharp and short and make you read in a quick staccato way.

> The thorns jab my arm,

> my leg, my cheek.

Other words roll off the tongue and you linger on them, reading them more slowly.

> The sunlight meandered over to my hammock

> and filled the afternoon with laziness.

HOW POEMS SOUND

Many people think poetry should sound a particular way. Certainly, in many poems, the poet doesn't make a statement directly, as he or she would in prose. In fact, poets often use comparisons such as metaphors and similes, in which two disparate ideas or images are juxtaposed. Many poets spend time working on how their poems sound. They use *alliteration, assonance,* and *consonance.* (See Glossary.) They purposely use words together that contain vowels or consonants that echo each other, such as "mornings mimic", "clean stream," or "sip and slurp." But the use of these poetic devices is not a requirement. Some poets don't think about sound as much as ideas. Some poets startle you with their directness. Poetry has no boundaries.

> "I think that we young poets approach poetry with a sense of what it is 'supposed' to sound like; there should be comparisons, and flowers, and showy words, and Love, and so on. The easiest trap to fall into is imitating that poetic tone, which can often lead to hollow or clichéd gestures. My advice is to ignore those notions of how poetry should sound, and write as honestly and personally as possible."
> —*Brian Laidlaw*

4 READING AND TALKING ABOUT A POEM WITH STUDENTS

READING POEMS ALOUD

Reading a poem aloud is an effective way to explore it. But how should a poem be read? Poems are divided into lines and verses (stanzas) and the poet has divided them in a particular way for a reason. When reading a poem, you can read it like prose, but make tiny pauses between lines and between stanzas because the poet broke the lines for this purpose. If you need to err between pausing too long at the line break and reading naturally as if the poem were prose, err on the side of reading naturally. The meaning of the poem will be clearer, and the listener won't be distracted by long pauses. And don't forget to read the title. It's an integral part of the poem.

> "To be a poet, you should read a lot of poetry as well as write it.
> Memorize some of your favorite poems so that they become part
> of your respiration, your breathing in and out. Speak your favorite
> poems out loud."
> —*Jane Yolen*

TALKING ABOUT POEMS

It's enough to read a poem aloud without analyzing it at all. Seriously. But it can also be fun and beneficial to let students talk about their favorite parts, to speculate on what the poem means, to notice how the poet plays with words—all in moderation.

When I first painted and wrote poetry, I didn't care what other people thought my work meant. It only meant what I intended it to mean. But then I realized that sometimes people noticed things about my work that I didn't even know were there. So I decided it was good to get feedback, and it was okay to look at other people's poems and make conjectures about what was happening in them.

Encourage students to try pointing out what they liked or disliked, even discussing some of the possibilities for what the poet meant, if they're so inclined. It takes concentration to discuss a poem since a lot of meaning is packed into a few words. It's like a guessing game or puzzle that has no correct answer. Your students' responses will show you where they empathize with the poem.

SUGGESTED QUESTIONS FOR DISCUSSING POETRY

If you and your students enjoy talking about poems, you can talk about a poem in different ways, such as:

- Does anything stand out as unusual, or different in the poem?
- What does the mood seem to be—angry, joyous, mournful, depressed, silly, contemplative?
- What is the poet's tone—sarcastic, serious, gentle, instructional, menacing, soothing, joking?
- How does the poem look on the page?
- What are your favorite words or phrases?
- Which words sound good together?
- How does the poet break the lines? Are they short or long lines? Are the breaks at natural pauses or not?
- How strong are the beginning and ending of the poem?
- Was something surprising in the poem? What?
- Were there parts you didn't understand or didn't like? Where?
- What do you think the poem might mean? What could it be about? (I always ask for other interpretations after the first student makes a comment to show that there isn't just one interpretation.)
- Does the poem have different layers? Is it about one obvious subject and another not-so-obvious, deeper subject?
- Have you ever felt the way the poet does?

It's worth mentioning that a poem often has several layers. It can be about the habits of a cat, and at the same time, be about the idea that curiosity can lead you to adventures that in turn might lead you to trouble. A poem can be about the poet's feelings at the end of summer and, at the same time, be about the way the poet has played with words in the poem and the way the poem sounds when you read it aloud.

It's okay to get a feeling from a poem without understanding every line. Sometimes a poem can make you laugh or cry or feel less alone, or it can help you notice something you've never noticed before. Sometimes a poem is just fun to read aloud because of the sounds.

Don't discuss poems for too long. But at the same time, let students say what they need to say about them. It can make them aware of poetic elements, such as metaphor, wordplay, line breaks and layers of meaning, all of which can help students with their own writing.

A stereotyped English teacher is one who analyzes a poem until the students are exasperated and have lost their enthusiasm for it. Former poet laureate Billy Collins even wrote a poem about this subject, "Introduction to Poetry." (See Bibliography, Free Verse, page 110.) To counter this tendency, I keep discussions relaxed, student-focused, and short (shorter than my example read-throughs) to capitalize on students' initial, visceral reactions to a poem.

SEQUENCE OF A LESSON

When I begin lessons in classrooms I visit, I pass out copies of the poem I'm using as an example and then show it on the overhead projector. Students can see the line breaks and every word of the poem as I read the poem aloud, or as a student reads it. Occasionally, I have the whole group read it aloud together. Then I ask some of the questions listed on page 16, if they seem engaged, or to engage them. I don't over-analyze by asking every question for every poem. I like to keep our discussions to 5 minutes maximum. If I notice something they didn't, I might add that to the discussion. Sometimes we just talk about what parts we liked best and what the poem was about.

When I'm asking students to write in a particular poetry form, we spend some time generalizing about the form. Presenting several poems in the same form can help students see the similarities and differences. We talk about the subject matter, the rhyme or rhythm, the number of stanzas or lines, and other features of the form. (The chapters in the second half of this book were written to supply helpful information in order for you to present sample poems and to discuss each poetry form in this way.)

Having a copy of the sample poem(s) for reference at their desks when they begin writing their own poetry can be beneficial for students. They can see how the poem is laid out on the page and note the characteristics of the poetry form being discussed. They can use the poem as a template, or a jumping-off place.

HOW POETS TALK ABOUT POETRY

In the following discussion, I've shown how poets might talk about three poems, one at the elementary level and two at the middle school/high school level. Until I went to a college course in which the professor unpacked a poem, I didn't know how to do it.

At the beginning of a unit on poetry, you might want to show students how I talked about one or all of these poems. These read-throughs can give students models of what aspects of a poem might be discussed when they talk about poetry. However, in most classroom situations, the students would be contributing their ideas, and the discussions might be shorter.

This poem by Kris Aro McLeod tells how to paint a summer day. Kris is a talented, published poet. She is also an artist, so she knows about painting first hand. Her poem is a list poem because she provides a list of instructions, written one after the other. To emphasize the structure of a list, she places the word "use" at the beginning of each line.

Read-through Example 1

Painting a Summer Day

use breezy blue
and fluffy white
use deep, warm yellow
use clear, use bright

use open windows
use cats asleep
use leafy shadows on concrete

use splashes, sprinkles, climbing trees
strawberries, melons, fat green peas

but never, ever use plain gray
to paint a lovely summer day.

—Kris Aro McLeod

She starts the poem with colors, something I might expect as a reader. But she includes the description, "breezy blue," which has great alliteration, and isn't an adjective that I normally hear in a description of the color blue. "Deep, warm yellow" gives a nice warm feeling. Then she starts surprising me by saying "use clear, use bright." It seems like she's warning the reader that she's not going to be traditional anymore.

My favorite stanza is the second one. The images are original and give a picture of summer. I really start to feel like it's summer when the windows are left open.

In the third stanza, she creates an interesting summer list that includes sounds that are fun to say: "splashes, sprinkles." She uses the sound of *e* over and over, the short sound and the long sound: "trees," "strawberries," "melons," "green peas."

She surprises me at the end by reversing the premise and talking about what not to use—"gray!"

The tone and mood of the poem seem light and cheerful but earnest. She achieves this by her crisp lines, her sparkly vocabulary, and her choice of uplifting images.

Kris doesn't use any unnecessary words and doesn't distract the reader by capitalizing the first letters of words that begin lines. Every item feels to me that it has equal weight, and they all add up to a summer's day.

And don't forget, she made the poem unusual from the start by talking about "painting a summer day." This might mean literally painting a picture on canvas or how nature paints a summer day or how to paint a summer day in the mind of the reader. This is an unusual way to approach a list poem about summer.

Read-through Example 2

New Honesty (excerpt)

Can I find a balance
between me and
the box I call my family?
I want equilibrium.
I want change.
I want to tell the Truth,
not the truth of the woman
who snapped on a collar
and named me alive.
Like a plastic ball,
I toss between myself
and the various identities
I have been assigned.
Look out—I fell in the mud.
Look out—I opened my mouth,
and out came ideas
you don't think are pretty.
I suppose it would be scary
to be a ventriloquist who found out
her dummy can talk,
to find the doll had a brain
and opinions that will bite
when provoked.
I suppose it would be scary
if I opened my coat
and showed you all my secrets.
Would you call me a flasher
and file charges?
Would you gaze blindly
refusing to see the Truth:
I'm sorry to tell you
that I'm not sorry anymore.
I can only run for so long
and so far.
I'm done,
and I'm throwing up my Truth
like a marathon runner
at the end
of a 16-year race.

—Jessie Childress

Jessie Childress is a skillful, powerful poet who has several poems in *Things I Have to Tell You, poems and writing by teenage girls* (Franco 2001). The poem "New Honesty" appears in that book in its entirety. In the read-through below, I am focusing on part of the poem, from line 11 to the end.

"New Honesty" is a free verse poem. It is about a personal subject, which is typical for this form. Jessie broke the lines where she felt a break made sense, and she created her own rhythm. There is no rhyme.

Her poem, written when she was 16, seems to be about self-discovery and finally speaking up and saying who you really are to your parent(s), no matter the consequences.

The poem is filled with striking images and comparisons. My favorite lines are:

> "I suppose it would be scary
>   to be a ventriloquist who found out
>   her dummy can talk,"

> "if I opened my coat
>   and showed you all my secrets.
>   Would you call me a flasher
>   and file charges?"

The images/metaphors are perfect for the situations she's describing. In both of the sections above, the fact that she carries the metaphor for quite a few lines helps hammer her points home. And the images bring out the tone of the poem, which I read as angry and rageful, yet confident.

The question mark is an intriguing device to use in the middle of the poem. It also adds emphasis.

> "Would you call me a flasher and file charges?"

I felt her shifting between empathizing with her parent and understanding her parent's point of view ("I suppose it would be scary") to adamantly saying she has to hold her ground ("I'm done,").

When she uses short choppy words in a row, I can feel the force of what she's saying.

> "Look out—I fell in the mud.
>   Look out—I opened my mouth,
>   and out came ideas
>   you don't think are pretty."

Then she slows it down and hits hard, with longer, more drawn out words.

> "I suppose it would be scary
>   to be a ventriloquist who found out
>   her dummy can talk,"

The way Jessie broke the three lines above shows the power of the line break. Each line builds tension and entices the reader to the next line, until the thought is finally completed. The third line was surprising and powerful when I got there.

This is free verse, so Jessie varies the rhythm in the poem. It's easy to read if I follow the line breaks. She seems to vary the lengths of the lines depending on what she wants to emphasize.

> "I can only run for so long
> and so far.
> I'm done,
> and I'm throwing up my Truth
> like a marathon runner
> at the end
> of a 16-year race."

The poem ends on another strong metaphor of a 16-year marathon. I like how she says she's "throwing up" her truth, which I took to mean that she's regurgitating it and/or tossing it in the air for all to see.

Read-through Sample 3

He Shaved His Head

> He shaved his head to release his imagination.
> He did it to get a tattoo on his shiny head.
> He did it to lose his normality.
> He did it to become a freak.
> He did it because he was angry.
> He did it to make people angry.
> He did it for himself.
> —Rene Ruiz

Rene Ruiz was 13 when he wrote this compelling poem as a participant in the Writers in the Schools (WITS) drop-in writing program in Houston, Texas. The workshops were set up for students of high school age. This poem appears in *You Hear Me? poems and writing by teenage boys* (Franco 2000).

I chose this poem because the form, a list poem, is very accessible, but Rene shows how pure honesty can capture your total attention. The poem is straightforward, but subtle.

His poem is so original—the images are fresh and imaginative. He starts with an image that immediately opens my mind:

> "He shaved his head to release his imagination."

The second image is just as striking because it brings me back to earth and surprises me.

"He did it to get a tattoo on his shiny head."

I feel a tone of anger building in the next lines, even though he's restrained and straightforward in his language.

> "He did it to become a freak.
> He did it because he was angry.
> He did it to make people angry."

The last line is perfect, getting to the heart of why he shaved his head.

> "He did it for himself."

To me, this poem speaks for any gesture of protest or any act that a person takes to declare his or her individuality or to fight against the norm, the system.

I like that the poem is centered on the page. It makes me notice the shape of the poem, particularly that the last line is the shortest, yet the strongest in a sense. The poem floats in the middle of the page, and the white space around it seems to frame it.

For me, this poem shatters the stereotype that teenage boys are all about anger, and anger alone. Rene reveals his subtle thoughts and feelings and shows how complex he is. The content of the poem is almost a metaphor for what poetry is all about. Poetry is about looking closely at something and making discoveries about yourself and/or what you're writing about. In this poem, an act that could be classified as a superficial fashion statement becomes so much more. It becomes a statement of individuality—a declaration of independence.

5 THE VALUE OF TEACHER DEMONSTRATION

At a session I attended during an annual reading conference, Donald Graves said that demonstrating writing in front of the students was the secret to creating a learning environment in the writing classroom. He went on to say that many teachers still don't demonstrate writing. That statement made me wonder why teachers resist the demonstrations that Donald Graves described. I explored some of the barriers that might arise when teachers consider writing poetry in front of their students. Some teachers might feel uncomfortable demonstrating something they are unfamiliar with. Some might not want to look as if they were unskillful at something. Others might feel it was too time-consuming. Others might be anxious about accessing their own creativity. The suggestions throughout the chapter address ways to overcome these barriers. They can be used to help student poets as well.

VALUE EACH WRITER'S PROCESS INCLUDING YOUR OWN

Just like your students, you have a story to tell, and there's no right way to do it. Every writer's process is different. For example, when I'm writing poetry, I like to write a very rough draft just to get something on paper, even if this first version is raw. Then I dig in and work on the verbs and banish the clichés, think about what I'm trying to say, and question the feeling the poem engenders. I start with an event or image that tickles or intrigues me. Sometimes I start with a phrase that sounds good to my ear.

But many of my poet friends take different approaches when they begin writing. Read their responses.

> "I start roughly. I write down whatever I think of; a billion ideas and words. Then I look for patterns and surprises. Then little by little the poem starts to form."
> —*Rebecca Kai Dotlich*

> "The building materials themselves: the words or the rhythm fuel my poems as frequently as the content does."
> —*Bobbi Katz*

> "When I'm lucky, it just comes to me. In those moments I will usually hear lines echoing in my head and I'll feel compelled to write them

down . . . But more and more I've been realizing that 95 percent of the time you have to make yourself write...that getting to the point where it will be good is inevitably going to be a process."
—Miriam Stone

"I start with a line, an image, a fragment and I write it down in long-hand before I forget it. . . . Sometimes a line of song will touch it off..."
—Mel Glenn

"Sometimes I'll be taking a walk or riding my bicycle and have an idea for a poem, and work it almost completely out in my head before I get home . . . I also get ideas from the poems I read . . ."
—Bob Grumman

"Sometimes, the poems just pop into my head while I'm reading; other times, I start with a theme and just play with words until I like what I hear."
—Katie McAllaster Weaver

"Sometimes I decide the poem will be in a form, such as a haiku or cinquain or triolet, and I look at what that form should be and think about syllables, end rhymes, rhythm before I begin."
—Marilyn Singer

"There have been many occasions where I have walked out of parties because inspiration had struck like lightening and I had to listen to it in order to get it out."
—Stephan Johnson

The point is that everyone's process suits him or her, and yours will suit you. Each of your students will also approach writing in a different way. It's as simple as respecting your process, and theirs as well.

EXPECT PROGRESS, NOT PERFECTION

One thing that I find encouraging in my work as a poet is visiting museums and finding the early paintings of famous artists such as Cezanne and Matisse. These early works usually aren't as polished as their later paintings. This gives me hope not only that my poems will improve over time, but also that my drafts will improve. I sometimes write three drafts, but often there are eight or even twenty drafts of the same poem. The early paintings of the masters also show me why it's important to keep writing all the time, and they encourage me to start where I am and progress from there. "Progress, not perfection" is a maxim I try to remember.

EMBRACING DEMONSTRATION

After thinking deeply about teachers' demonstrations in front of the class, I've come to the conclusion that it's asking a lot, but that the payback for the students is worth the risk and the time. Even if the teacher isn't a great poet, the students deserve to be shown how to write a poem because it helps them tremendously to see the process. No one but you is available to show them this process. And it can take as little as five minutes a session.

To get over some of the natural hurdles, I've brainstormed some suggestions, alternatives, and hints.

Use one of my demonstrations in front of the class to get your feet wet. To help you understand how I thought about each poetry form, I included a section called a "think- through" in which I explain in detail how I wrote one of the sample poems. These sixteen written demonstrations in Section II can help you get started with your own, give you some insight into what a first draft can look like in raw form, and show you how to proceed through the revision stages.

- Write a poem at home, keeping all your drafts. Then reconstruct it in the classroom. When I go to a classroom as a guest poet, this is what I do. I write the poem beforehand and show the students the process, starting with my first thoughts and my first drafts.
- As a teacher, trust in your ability to be spontaneous, something you do every day. Be honest with the students about your experience with writing poetry.
- As you're writing, let the students make suggestions, but take only the suggestions you like. The demonstration poem is yours; it's not a collaborative poem.

GETTING A GRIP ON "THE JUDGE"

I think the barriers to demonstrating in front of the class—and for some students to write poetry at all—often relate back to what I call "the judge." There is a voice in my head and in many writers' heads that criticizes. It has discouraging things to say, such as, "You're not a good enough writer. You don't know what you're doing. You're going to show that to someone?" Even after twenty-five years of writing, my judge is still like a broken record. I'm just used to it. Luckily, my judge goes to sleep while I'm writing but it comes out in full force when I'm physically trying to mail a manuscript to an editor.

If yours comes out while you're writing, it's best to tell it to come back later when you're in the revising stage. Tell it you'd like to write alone. Then suspend all judgment of your writing. This works for students who are having trouble getting started as well.

> "Of course, there is always the voice that says what you've written is totally banal, get rid of it; you think you're a writer? That is the voice you have to seriously squelch."
> —*Mel Glenn*

> "I try to stuff a sock into that little judge's mouth and tell her to shut it! . . . If you listen to that voice you will never write anything, or if you do manage to get something out you will only be writing what you think other people will want to read, and not necessarily what speaks to you most, what comes from your soul."
> —*Miriam Stone*

". . . [I hear] every negative voice you can imagine. So I tell myself I'm just doing this for fun."
—*Maria Damon*

"Ah, the voices. With poetry, the "judge" is often quiet. But I think reading out loud helps drown out the negative voices, so you can really just listen to the heart of the poem."
—*Katie McAllaster Weaver*

"Actually I like my little judge. It says, 'That ain't gonna work' or 'Damn good poem!' I trust it."
—*Marilyn Singer*

SUSPENDING JUDGMENT

Some methods I use to relax and suspend judgment are:

- I write by hand, or I write my first draft on the computer, whichever gets me out of my analytical self that day.
- I write somewhere away from my desk, such as the dining room table or a café.
- I write on a walk, with a pad and pencil.
- I write when I'm swimming and jot down the poem on a pad in my purse when I emerge from the water.
- I write in the bathroom!
- I take notes before I start writing.
- I ask the universe for help so I'm not doing it alone.
- I tell myself I'm helping kids with my writing.
- I talk to myself as if I'm a mother or father talking to a child, encouraging her to write whatever she wants.
- I tell myself I have a story to tell, just like everyone else.
- I tell myself it's always good to take risks.
- I talk back to my voices. Here are some retorts that might be useful to you:

Voice	Rebuttal
"The kids will think I can't write."	"Actually the kids will be eager to get to know me better."
"I don't have the skills to write a poem."	"There will be students who can relate and will see me taking a chance. Besides, I am bound to improve over time."
"I'll seem silly."	"Actually I'm going to seem generous and adventurous."

Voice	Rebuttal
"I don't write well in front of people."	"I can write the poem at home and bring in my notes and drafts."
"I don't have a clue where to start."	"I'm going to start with Betsy Franco's demos in Section II and then try one of my own."
"They don't really need to see me writing a poem."	"I remember when someone demonstrated how something was done. What a relief it was to see someone going through the steps. It gave me confidence."
"Why put myself through this?"	"I won't know which students will benefit greatly from this unless I try it. It's always beneficial and exciting to take a risk."

ONCE WHEN I BALKED

Imagine how I felt when I was asked to speak about my teen anthologies at a juvenile hall for boys. At first I resisted. I told the librarian who had invited me that I had never done anything like that, and, besides, what did I know? Then I told myself it was worth it if one boy heard something from me that he needed to hear.

It turned out to be one of the most uplifting book talks I've ever given. Nothing happened the way I expected. The boys took turns reading the poetry from my anthology out loud, they wrote their own poems, they shared their work. They didn't like the sample poem I had picked as a possible model. We dropped it, and they wrote what they wanted to write—about jail and life outside of jail. I was shocked. I was so glad I had taken the risk.

I think you'll be surprised by the results if you are someone who has been resistant to demonstrating in class. In the same vein, your students who get over the hurdle and start to write poetry will surprise themselves by how much they have to say.

6 WARM-UPS AND POETRY STARTERS

My writing motor clicks in every morning. I wake up at 5:30 A.M., and I can write immediately in the quiet, new morning, before anyone but the cats are up. But I've noticed that many writers need to warm up first.

> "Most of the time I think it's easiest to just start writing anything—just whatever you happen to be thinking about that day—and eventually you'll get into the mindset where you can write with some clarity and poetic style, and you may write a few lines that you like. And then you have the beginning of a poem."
> —*Miriam Stone*

> "How do I get started? I procrastinate. I read the newspaper; I write emails; I see what's on TV—anything not to write. It is hard. As Dorothy Parker says, 'I love having written.' Whoever tells you writing is fun is lying through their teeth."
> —*Mel Glenn*

> "Ideas for poems are all around us. All we have to do is quiet down enough to let ourselves observe and feel. There are many more poems than we could possibly write just waiting for us to give them lives!"
> —*Bobbi Katz*

> "I walk around outside, with a piece of paper, until something strikes me. It usually doesn't take more than fifteen minutes before I see a trigger of some kind. . . ."
> —*Brian Laidlaw*

HELPFUL TOPICS

I almost always make a list of general topics available to students so that they aren't searching in their brains and coming up with nothing. Here are my favorites:

    nature
    seasons
    animals
    school
    friends
    family
    sports

food
feelings
memories
hobbies
world news

For older students add:

relationships
social issues
justice
personal struggles
gender

WARM-UP EXERCISES

To get the gears moving and the pencils flowing, here are a few suggestions. Students can write in prose or poetry to warm up. Encourage them just to write without thinking too hard. For example:

- Write about what has happened so far this morning.
- Write about what happened in the last five minutes.
- Write about what you see around you.
- Think about your five senses and write what you hear, see, taste, touch, and/or smell.
- Write about something that is making you happy, sad, or angry.
- Write three words you like. Using those words, write without thinking.
- Write for five minutes without thinking or stopping.
- Look around the room and find a phrase or a sentence written somewhere. Use that to write a line of poetry. [Note: Collecting these and reading them aloud as a collaborative poem can be very effective.]
- Pretend you are your pet or your father/mother. What would you say this morning?
- Pretend you're an ant lost in the classroom.

You might want to demonstrate a warm up exercise in front of students to show them what you mean. For example:

A Dog's Morning

I heard my person's alarm.
I stretched my back legs, one at a time.
I stretched my front legs.
I yawned till my jaw was as wide as it gets.
I scratched at my person's bedroom door
and heard her yawning.
I led her down the hall to my dog dish.
She understood and fed me.
I chomped on my food and
took a drink from the toilet.
I found her at her desk

and curled up on her foot.
Time to sleep for a while after all that activity.

I carry a word bowl with me when I visit classrooms. It's filled with strips of paper with nouns, verbs, adjectives, and adverbs that can spark the imagination. Here are some words to get your word bowl started:

shadows, mashed potatoes, iguana, peanut butter, crystal, darkness
zoom, shove, scamper, tiptoe, swing, wrestle, drift
curious, rusty, lumpy, rotten, velvety, prickly, peaceful
shyly, noisily, silently, bravely, carelessly, dangerously

Each student could suggest a word to add to the bowl. The way it works: a student takes three words out of the bowl without looking and uses some or all of the words she likes to get started.

This technique can also be expanded to an "idea bowl" or "object bowl" that you can keep adding to. When teaching in workshops, the poet Mel Glenn does something similar with ideas like dog food, jeans, deodorant, fast food restaurant, new TV show, loneliness, Saturday, three wishes, nightmares, plans for the future, braces, my pet, and so on. He makes a numbered list of ideas. The students pick a number and write about the topic on the list that corresponds to the number.

Anything that can get students in the present with their pencils moving is helpful. Sometimes changing the topic for writing helps.

> "There are times I simply cannot come up with a poem. I recently tried and tried to write a poem about the moon for one of my own collections, *Sky Magic*. I stayed up nights to look at the moon in its various shapes. I looked at the moon at various places where I live . . . I literally begged the moon to bring me something . . . some words, some magic. Nothing came. I gave up on the project after months. The moon and I just couldn't get it together. Several days later I penned a poem about the sunset! The moon didn't work but the sun shone!"
> —*Lee Bennett Hopkins*

Just like warming up a car or warming up your brain on a Monday morning, it can make all the difference to start with a "throw-away" exercise. It can serve as a transition and wake up the creative parts of students' minds.

7 REVISION AS EXPERIMENTATION

Revision is a word with an unpleasant connotation for many students and adults. It implies that the first draft is bad and needs to be fixed. It brings to mind drudgery, hard work and getting down to business. *Experimenting with a poem* has a much more positive, adventurous ring to it. I like to think of revision in the spirit of experimentation. In my Think-throughs in Section II, you will find examples of how I "experiment" with my poems, from start to finish.

In this vein, I like to keep my first draft intact on the computer and make a copy of it that I use for revising. I do this because it's hard to tear something apart, particularly if I'm attached to it. This is especially true for students. So I call revising an experiment, with myself and with students. I tell them what I tell myself, that they can always change their poem back to its original form.

Poet and novelist Miriam Stone taught me that I don't need to worry about the destroying the heart of the poem in the revision stages. Here's what she said:

> "In a typical first draft I may have one or two lines that end up being
> worth saving. But the cool thing is that those lines often end up be-
> ing the backbone of the final poem, so nothing is really wasted."
> —*Miriam Stone*

If students wonder if poets revise, listen to this:

> "I feel a poem has to be worked on like a piece of sculpture, chipping
> away at every fold. This means eliminating as many words as one
> can, for poetry should hinge on each and every word."
> —*Lee Bennett Hopkins*

> "Revising is a little bit like wringing out a wash cloth. I know that a
> poem is finished when I can't squeeze any more water out of it."
> —*Bobbi Katz*

> "Every poem I write goes through 10-20 revisions. Shelley allegedly
> wrote 'Ozymandias' in one sitting. If so, astonishing. I've not
> been so fortunate, and quite obviously, I am not even writing
> 'Ozymandias.'"
> —*J. Patrick Lewis*

> "I begin my poems by scratching out a phrase or image, and that of-
> ten triggers my imagination . . . Those lines that might have helped
> me get started,—ah, I feel guilt—might be abandoned in the end."
> —*Gary Soto*

REVISION/EXPERIMENTATION IDEAS

With older students, I hand out and discuss the list of ideas and suggestions below. They pick and choose from the list to revise/experiment with their poems. With intermediate students, we might focus on several of the revision ideas in one session. With younger students, I ask them to experiment in simple ways. I might suggest that they experiment by changing one word in their poem to a more interesting word, knowing that they can always change it back.

What would happen if you—

- change some words to more interesting words?
- change some verbs to stronger verbs?
- take out some words that are unnecessary?
- get rid of clichés, or phrases you've heard before?
- put in some of the senses, such as smells and sounds?
- take out or change lines that don't fit the rhythm or the idea of the poem?
- try a new title?
- change the beginning?
- change the ending?
- change the mood or tone (e.g. from sad to angry)?
- change the point of view?
- switch some lines around?
- experiment with different line breaks?
- use details instead of being general?
- use memories, real experiences?

The purpose of revising/experimenting is to help the poem say what the poet really wants it to say: for the poem to be itself more; for the poem to be energetic, alive, specific; clear or unclear (whichever the poet wants); and as fresh as it can be.

"I WONDER" QUESTIONS

Below are some questions that a poet can ask herself/himself in the spirit of experimentation. These ideas embellish and extend the more concise list above:

"I wonder what would happen if I . . ."

- changed one word to a more interesting word?
  silky versus *soft*
- took out one word from every line?
- took out unnecessary words?
- added an adverb?
  carelessly   lazily   timidly
- made three verbs more exact?

barged versus *ran,* *slinked* versus *walked,* *sprang* versus *jumped*

- changed one phrase that sounds like something I've heard before?
  as ferocious as a cornered ferret is better than *as ferocious as a lion*
- took out a line that is very general and substituted a detailed example?
  > *cleaned up my room* versus
  > *stuffed my books,*
  > *my tattered comics,*
  > *and my smelly soccer gear*
  > *into the farthest corner*
  > *under the bed*
- made every line twice as long?
  > *wove his web* versus
  > *wove geometric shapes of uncanny precision*
- changed the line breaks so the lines were shorter or longer?
- did not break a line where the natural pause fell?
  > *I tumbled off the*
  > *roof and sprained my*
  > *ankle*
- switched the order of some lines?
- let the person next to me add a line to my poem?
- read the poem backwards?
- changed the last line to make it more surprising, strong?
- removed the last line?
- thought of two new titles?
- illustrated it?
- cut it up and made it a collage?
- added a sound effect?
- added images having to do with the five senses: hearing, seeing, touching, tasting, and smelling?
  > *Monday after a vacation*
  > *tastes like sour milk that's*
  > *clotted into clumps.*
- wrote the poem again backwards under the original poem?
- turned it into a visual poem?
- changed the speaker in the poem from "I" to "you," "she," or "he?"
- wrote the poem in the past, present, or future tense?
- changed words to change the mood?
  > *Oh, brother, I won't do that again.*
  > has a different mood than
  > *I felt like I'd turned myself inside-out*
  > *and everyone was staring*
- ended with a question?

- rewrote the poem without any rhymes, or only internal rhymes?

Another major tool for revision is to read a poem aloud or have someone else read it aloud. Then the poet can ask herself or himself:

- Where does it stumble?
- Are some lines unnecessary?
- Is something unclear? Do I care?
- Does it have a rhythm of its own? Do any lines break the rhythm? Is that okay?

> "Sometimes in writing a poem I get stuck for a word for days, weeks even. Maybe longer. I read the poem aloud, think about the rhythm, the lyrical line, about each word and how it works with the words before and after. Does a word echo (not rhyme exactly) another key word? Have I put down an overused phrase. Am I clear in what I am saying, even though I am speaking metaphorically? Is there true emotion contained within the poem?"
> —Jane Yolen

CLARITY OR NOT?

For many types of writing, the author wants to be clear and consistent. For poetry this isn't always necessary. In poetry, sometimes ambiguity is interesting. A poet might leave out a clarifying comma, period, or word to keep the reader guessing.

> anger memories
> pounding in my mind
> as I shuffle through
> my feet demolish the leaves

Try putting a period after the word *mind,* or after the word *through*—the poem reads differently, but either way makes sense. Because the narrator is angry, there are no commas or periods and things aren't as clear as they might be.

A break in the rhythm of a poem can signal a change in mood or a change in the situation.

> Storm thrashing and flashing
> Wind billowing and blustering
> One last clap of thunder.
> It's over.

Or a change in rhythm can keep the poem from sounding too sing-songy.

Poems don't always make sense. The surrealist poets purposely made poetry that didn't make sense to the logical mind. The sounds might make sense to the ear or the mind, might be tickled to think about something that tweaks the imagination. The cinquain below is an example of this. If you loosen your logical mind from its moorings, it's fun to read.

Cinquain

Breathing,
like paper trash
in an unexpected wind storm,
can seem more like the moon than a
cat's eye.

There's also the fact that poetry can be written with an audience in mind, or it can be written just for the poet. There are times the poet doesn't care about being perfectly clear. The poem can be a way to express feelings or insights, in order to process them and put them in a concrete form, for only the poet's eyes. Even a poem that will be read by others is often written just for the poet.

"I write for myself, an audience of one. This is one of the reasons, I suppose, that I don't write verse for the very young. I don't want to be hemmed in with so many vocabulary constraints."
—J. Patrick Lewis

"I write for myself. But I am a very dedicated reader and read many different things. So I am the perfect audience for what I write!"
—Jane Yolen

"I try to write my poems for myself, but once I begin adapting them into songs, the audience becomes much more of a concern."
—Brian Laidlaw

"I always, always have children in mind. Children. Not an age . . . I write with the same joys and excitement that I felt as a child, slipping my own memories in and around it all."
—Rebecca Kai Dotlich

WORKSHOPPING

"I like to get a first draft of a poem or story quickly, and then I go back to hone the writing. I then share the work with my wife, who acts as my editor. No one works alone."
—Gary Soto

Many teachers incorporate revision conferences/workshops into their classrooms: between the teacher and the student, between the class and the student, or in small groups or partners. This technique is similar to what some poets call workshopping. It's what I do in my writing group which consists of five children's book writers. Note that some students will work best one-on-one with you or a partner because they are overly sensitive to feedback.

With all student poetry, the most important thing is to be positive. (See Chapter 8 on Assessing Poetry Poetically.) Students will need to be taught how to ask questions and make suggestions positively. In my own writing group, I suggested that they first tell me what was working before giving me suggestions about what to consider changing in my drafts.

The language that is helpful sounds like this:

Positive Feedback:

- The key lines seem to be "_____." Do you agree?
- Your opening really grabs my attention.
- The phrase "_____" made me interested.
- The ending surprised me.
- The words "_____" were powerful and unusual. They really gave me a picture in my mind.
- The poem made me feel _____ and it made me think _____.
- This poem was so interesting, memorable, unusual because _____.

Clarifying Questions:

- I thought your poem was about _____. Is that right? If not, could you tell me more about your poem?
- I didn't quite understand what you meant by this part, "_____." Do you mind explaining that part to me?
- When you said, "_____," I was curious to know more detail.
- I would love to know more about what the person in your poem is like— what they look like, where they live, what their quirks are and what they like and dislike.
- You might want to experiment with sound effects or bringing in other senses since your subject matter is _____.
- I wonder what would happen if you shortened the lines.
- Have you thought about what would happen if you used the phrase _____ ____ less often or varied it?
- I wonder what would happen if you experimented with your verbs.

The writer might have some questions:

- I'm struggling with the beginning. Should I _____ or _____.
- Do you think the ending is strong enough?
- Does the word _____ work here?
- Should I give more detail about _____?
- Does the mood of _____ come across?

A poet is free to take suggestions or not. It's his or her poem. For some students, just writing the poem is a victory. For others, experimenting helps them grow in an arena they love. Others may take small steps by changing one word, improving one verb, taking out one word. And that's a victory, too.

8   ASSESSING POETRY POETICALLY

"Do not fear mistakes. There are none."
  —*Miles Davis*

Poetry is a fairly fragile mode of creativity, so for me, the words *assessment* and *poetry* don't go together. Although poetry is not always about emotions, the idea of assessing students' poetry in the traditional sense of the word is as fruitless as assessing someone's emotions. If someone says, "I feel sad because _____," you can't really assess, approve or disapprove of, or improve on his or her emotion.

BUILDING CONFIDENCE

When it comes to poetry, the revision/experimentation workshops have a place, with moderation, but evaluation and assessment don't. The terms *revision* and *experimentation* imply that the poet is in charge and knows the truth about his or her poem. The terms *evaluation* and *assessment* imply that the teacher is in charge and knows the truth about the poem. Evaluation and assessment can squelch a poet's spirit when what you're trying to build is confidence.

> "I'd like to suggest that the judgment model may be much less em-
> powering than it appears and may actually be debilitating."
> —*Stephen Healey*

Teachers and educators sometimes have the idea that they aren't doing their jobs if they don't evaluate, but in the case of poetry, all you really have to do is listen—listen to the poem and listen to what the student has to say about it. It's time to turn off every judging impulse, with regard to your students' poetry and your own. It's a time to relax and get excited and look for the newness, the uniqueness in language, content, and presentation. When Lee Bennett Hopkins is choosing poems for his classic anthologies, he must evaluate, but here's what he says:

> "It's quite simple. When I read a verse someone writes or has written,
> and I go 'Oooh!' and goose bumps take over my skin, I know it is the
> right poem for the collection I'm working on."
> —*Lee Bennett Hopkins*

You can focus on the positive aspect of any poem your students produce because the good news is that they are expressing themselves and trying new poetry forms. I like to play on students' strengths. My responses sound something like this:

- Would you be willing to tell me about your poem? I'm really interested to hear how you thought of it and what it means to you.
- This poem/line sounds so much like you.
- I learned a lot about you from that poem. Your honesty gave the poem its power.
- The phrase "summer sun swimming across the seas" is strong and beautiful and fun to say.
- The word *mysterious* is very fitting for a jellyfish.
- You really experimented with spacing on the page.
- You picked a very interesting and unusual topic.
- You seem to know a lot about black holes.

> "Your normal nature is nurturing, open, and warm, or you wouldn't be a teacher. For some reason, this sometimes closes down because of a lack of familiarity with poetry, making you more tentative and uncertain . . . Bring your warmth to the area of poetry."
> —Maria Damon

RISK-TAKING

Writing poetry is about taking a risk, not about being perfect—more so than in other forms of writing, from my perspective as a poet. Your students are taking a risk just by writing poetry on a regular basis. Of course, there's room for work-shopping, to whatever degree the student can handle, but leave assessment/final evaluations for some other aspect of the curriculum. If you must evaluate, do it on effort and progress and the degree of risk the student took, considering where he or she started, illustrated in the chart on page 41.

A NEW LOOK AT RUBRICS

I designed a rubric that suits my philosophy because I realize that some schools require rubrics on every paper that goes into a student's portfolio. I suggest using checkmarks, or the highest rubric, next to the appropriate category.

	Most powerful aspect	Aspect in which student took the most risk	Aspect that is most improved	Aspect student wants to focus on next
content				
meaning				
honesty				
tone or mood				
point of view				
word choice/ verbs				
use of specific detail				
use of the senses				
title				
beginning				
ending				
how the poem reads				
presentation of poem (visual or oral)				

9 WAYS TO PUBLISH AND PRESENT STUDENT WORK

Teachers have developed many creative ways to publish and perform poetry in the classroom. Making poetry "public" is certainly worth the time because it validates and shows respect for student work, and it simulates the real world of publishing. It also helps build a community of poets. (See Chapter 1.)

PUBLISHING IN THE CLASSROOM

Listed here are a number of ideas to try:

- Bind the poems of each student into a poetry collection.
- Create a class book using all the class poems written in a particular poetry form.
- Have students choose one poem, write the lines of the poem on the pages of a handmade book or accordion book, one line per page, and illustrate it.
- Create a poetry bulletin board or wall.
- Show older students a variety of ways to hand-bind their books.
- Make the lines of a poem hang from a mobile.
- Design poem posters.
- Create greeting cards with the poems inside.
- Create a web site and post student poems. Tell another class about it.
- Start a class literary magazine or have students submit to a school literary magazine.
- Put up large sheets of paper and have students write their poems on them as if they were murals or graffiti-filled walls.

HOW TO PERFORM POETRY

Performing poetry is another way to present it.

- Organize a poetry reading with a moderator who introduces each poet.
- Create a poetry party with refreshments and invite another class. This could include an "open mic" in which poets volunteer to read their work, poetry posters, and/or poetry displays.
- Have a talent show with some people presenting poetry.

There are many different ways to read poetry aloud. One way is to be very natural or even understated. Another is to make the reading more like a performance. I asked the best performance poet I know about performing her poetry.

Mahogany Foster is 26 and performs in the Bay Area and New York. I met her when she was in high school and included her in one of my anthologies *Things I Have to Tell You, poems and writing by teenage girls.* Following are excerpts from my interview with her about reading poetry to a group:

"It's important to remember that poetry is a very physical thing. You have to engage a lot of your body. Take the focus off the cerebral and focus on the words. I tell my students to throw their shoulders back and puff their chests out and hold their chins out."

"I recommend you take it very slow. You have the crowd's attention and every word you say is very important. In poetry you can't afford to run over words unless it's for cadence purposes."

"I like to play with people. Bring your tone way down and it can be very powerful. You add timber to your voice. You take timber out of your voice."

"I want people to feel the way I feel about the poem."

"Memorize, memorize. memorize. Then even if you're not a performance poet, you can be walking down the street and you can see the words anywhere."

"When I write a poem, it's everywhere. I see it. I hear it. There's a beat to it. When I was in New York it was the way people walk when they're getting off the subway and walking around. My poems from New York have a choppier rhythm. They have more of a beat."

"Poetry is everywhere."
— *Mahogany Foster*

PUBLISHING OUTSIDE THE CLASSROOM

For years, I have been compiling a list of places where students can submit work. However, you and your students should be aware of a few things. The first one is that it's not simple to get published. Students should consider it a major accomplishment just to submit their work. They should know that some of my manuscripts have taken eight to ten years to find a publisher, that my pile of rejections is a foot high, and that rejection is part of the process. The good news is that now my stack of published books has grown higher than my stack of rejections. Becoming published takes patience and persistence to the point of stubbornness.

The second is that some places take all rights to student poems. That means the student can never submit it anywhere else. I do not recommend that students give up all their publishing rights, but it's a personal choice.

The third is that you don't need to purchase a copyright. Just write © (student name) on the bottom of each page. Avoid publishing "opportunities" that require you to pay a fee and/or require you to purchase an expensive anthology.

WHERE STUDENTS CAN SUBMIT

Submit to Frodos Notebook at
http://www.frodosnotebook.com/submit.html. Ages 13-19.

Submit to *Poetic Voices,* an online poetry site at
http://www.poeticvoices.com/Guidelines.htm.
There is no age limit, but I would suggest 11 and up.

Cicada Magazine at
http:// www.cricketmag.com/pages_content.asp?page_id=22
Submissions Editor
P.O. Box 300
315 Fifth St.
Peru, IL 61354
Send a cover letter, SASE, and note how many words in each poem.
Submit no more than 3 poems at once. This magazine is for teenagers.

For Art and Writing Awards, see
http://www.scholastic.com/artandwritingawards/index.htm. Grades 7-12.

High school students can look in *Poets and Writers Magazine* for ads that ask for
submissions. For more information, see www.pw.org.

Submit to *Teen Ink Magazine*, an online monthly magazine at
http://www.teenink.com.
Note: They keep all rights to your work. Ages 13-19.

Stone Soup Magazine, http://www.stonesoup.com. Link at bottom of home page
says "Send Work." Ages: up to 13.

Submit to *Merlyn's Pen,* http://www.merlynspen.org/write/submit.php.
Ages 6-12.

Girls can submit to *New Moon Magazine*. For information see
http://www.newmoon.org. Ages 8-14.

Submit to *Potluck Literary Magazine* at
http://www.potluckmagazine.org. Ages 8-16.

This site will connect you with many other sites of magazines that publish
student work, some of which are listed above:
http://www.geocities.com/fifth_grade_tpes/publish.html.

10 SOME SUGGESTED LOGISTICS FOR TEACHING POETRY

Donald Graves and Lucy Calkins suggest that writing every day is important for developing effective writers. The poetry forms certainly fit into any daily writing program in elementary school. These forms could also be part of the writing curriculum in middle school and high school. Poetry writing increases students' facility with language, even when writing essays and other prose forms.

The general teaching plans presented in this chapter would certainly take more than one day unless you leave out some of the steps from time to time or assign some of it for homework. However, even at the upper grade levels, I suggest making time to write poetry *in class*, at least occasionally, because it creates an energy in the classroom that improves students' writing and helps build community.

On days when you present a particular poetry form, you could introduce the form using details from the background information provided for each chapter in Section II. Then you could present a sample poem or poems from Section II on an overhead or chart paper. It's also helpful, but not a necessity, to distribute a copy of the poem to each student or pair of students. It can be very useful for students to have a copy to refer to during discussions and again while writing poetry in the same form. Each lesson includes a bibliography directing you to other sample poems, in books and online, to expand students' understanding of the form. These poems can also be presented.

Students could spend about 5-10 minutes making observations about the poems—what lines or words they particularly like, how the poem affects them, what they think the poet is saying. (See page 16). They could make some generalizations about the form, especially if you present more than one poem. Either way, you'll probably have to point out some of the features of each poetry form.

Next, it's time for a poetry-writing demonstration. (See Chapter 5 and Think-throughs in Section II). Write a poem of your own in the form you're focusing on, either by writing in front of the class or bringing in a poem you've worked on outside of class. Some days, writing a collaborative poem with the whole class will get everyone involved. Some days, a writing warm up is just what's needed before students write their poems. (See Chapter 6).

After brainstorming some possible topics and/or putting the general list of poetry topics on page 29 on display, it's time for students to write their own poems. It can be useful to have elementary school students tell their neighbor the topic they've chosen to write about, knowing that they can always change it. This may take a few minutes of thought.

While students write, you can circulate and mini-conference with them, asking them to tell you about their poems—their topic, what they have so far, where they might be going. Some poets will want to be left alone. Writing can go on for 15-30 minutes.

Students may want to share some of their work during the writing session. This can be done formally or informally. Another ice-breaker idea is to have all students write down their best two lines. You can collect these and read them as one poem.

Revision/experimentation/workshopping conferences can take place at another time. These can involve the whole class, small groups, pairs of students, or you and the student. They can be held while students are doing other tasks. During these workshops, students can read their poems aloud and get positive feedback and "I wonder" questions from other students. (See pages 34-36.) Another option in the upper grades is for you or another student to give written feedback.

It can also be helpful to present particular revision/experimentation ideas to the whole class and have all students try the idea on their poems on the spot. For example, everyone could experiment with improving verbs. Students can also be given the list on page 34. They can try at least one or two experiments from the list, knowing that they can always change their poems back to the originals. Regardless of how this lesson is done, students will need time to revise their poems in class or at home. Computers may be available for students who want to type their work.

Once students have decided on a final version, you can create a forum for presenting their work. You can also provide a way for them to publish their poems after each form is completed or after a number of forms have been explored. (See Chapter 9.)

SCHEDULING POSSIBILITIES

Plan I

In this plan, days 1 and 2 could be combined to sustain the energy.

Day 1
introduce the form
pass out and display sample poems
read and discuss samples (5-10 minutes)
generalize about the structure and features of the poetry form

Day 2
demonstrate writing the form (5 minutes)
brainstorm ideas and post general topics (2 minutes)
allow time for students to write (15-30 minutes)

Day 3

revise/experiment as a whole class or individually
hold mini-conferences or organize workshops in small groups
allow time for further revision/experimentation
share

Day 4

share

Plan II

This plan is the one I follow when I give workshops at schools, except that a shortened revision/experimentation period and the sharing both take place that day.

Day 1

introduce the form
pass out and display sample poems
read and discuss samples (5-10 minutes)
generalize about the structure and features of the poetry form
demonstrate writing the form (5 minutes)
brainstorm ideas and post general topics (2 minutes)
allow time for students to write (15-30 minutes)
mini-conference with students as you're circulating
assign revision/experimentation for homework, sending home the list on page xx

Days 2-5

allow a few students at a time to share

Plan III

Day 1

introduce the form
pass out and display sample poems
read and discuss samples (5-10 minutes)
generalize about the structure and features of the poetry form
demonstrate writing the form (5 minutes)
brainstorm ideas and post general topics (2 minutes)
begin student writing (10 minutes)
complete student writing at home

Day 2

mini-conference or organize workshopping groups.
Have students complete revisions at home.

Day 3

share

11 INTRODUCING THE POETRY FORMS

"Many young writers like writing poetry in form because it gives
them some sort of boundary in their writing . . ."
—*Paul Janeczko*

After reading teaching standards from a variety of states, I chose 16 poetry forms for grades K through 12 to include in this book. I narrowed the list after studying a large body of specific poetry forms.

First, I wanted to include some familiar forms, such as haiku, limerick, and acrostic while, at the same time, introducing some forms that were less familiar, such as visual poetry, found poems, and multi-voice poems. I wanted to include some forms that would familiarize students with classic poems, such as old ballads. I also chose forms such as visual poetry and found poems that enabled me to include avant-garde poetry in the bibliography.

In contemplating the age range, from K-12, I made sure I had some forms, such as the list poem, acrostic, riddle, and diamanté that would appeal right away to primary teachers. I included blues poems, odes, and persona poems to appeal to intermediate teachers. The ballad, found poem, sonnet and sestina are a little more advanced, for middle school and high school teachers.

However, as you will discover, many of the forms can be adapted to all levels. For example, the list poem can be just as powerful for a kindergartner writing about her bicycle as for a high school senior writing about college applications. In addition, blues poems, free verse, and persona poems are appropriate for a wide range of students. Haiku can be taught nicely alongside the senryu and the renga in upper grades, and the double acrostic can be a real stretch. The cinquain is a challenging alternative to the diamanté. Thinking of the riddle as a paradox makes it interesting for older students.

I recommend all 16 poetry forms for middle school/high school, all but the sonnet and sestina for intermediate students, and all but the ballad, found poem, sonnet, and sestina for primary.

The poetry forms are listed below in order of accessibility.

Poetry Form	Primary	Intermediate	Middle/High School
List Poem	x	x	x
Acrostic	x	x	x
Riddle	x	x	x
Diamanté/Cinquain	x	x	x
Haiku, Senryu, and Renga	x	x	x
Visual Poetry	x	x	x
Free Verse	x	x	x
Limerick	x	x	x
Blues Poem	x	x	x
Ode	x	x	x
Persona Poem	x	x	x
Multi-Voice Poem	x	x	x
Ballad		x	x
Found Poem		x	x
Sonnet			x
Sestina			x

Now that you're armed with the tools you need to teach poetry, you will find Section II a useful resource for teaching 16 different poetry forms. For each form you'll find historical background and sample poems at multiple grade levels to get you started in the classroom. A "Think-through" for one of the poetry samples of each form provides inside information about my writing process, from choosing a topic to revising/experimenting with the poem. These Think-throughs help students think like writers and can be used as demonstrations. I hope they will make you feel more comfortable modeling your ideas and poetry writing in front of your students, telling your story and offering help to your students at the same time. Finally, bibliographies of poems and online sites for each of the 16 forms will fill out your poetry library and offer additional re-sources when teaching each form.

Now it's time to dive into teaching the forms and having students write their own poetry. You can use chapters on each poetry form in Section II in conjunction with the practical suggestions in Section I to build your own community of poets!

SECTION II

UNPACKING THE POETRY FORMS

12 ACROSTIC
Recommended for Grades K-12

BACKGROUND

The acrostic poem is an ancient poetry form. Acrostic poems were written in Babylonian, Greek, Latin, and Hebrew. In Hebrew, some of the Psalms are acrostics. Many early acrostics were based on the poet's name or on the name of the person addressed in the poem. Edgar Allan Poe wrote a famous acrostic to his valentine using the letters of her name on a diagonal in the poem.

CHARACTERISTICS OF AN ACROSTIC

- In an acrostic poem, the letters of a word(s), name, or phrase are written vertically down the page.
- These letters become the first letters of words, phrases, or sentences in each line of the poem.
- Lines in an acrostic poem can involve single words, phrases/sentences that are grammatically complete, or run-on lines of a poem.
- In a double acrostic, the beginning and ending letters of each line are part of the acrostic.
- Acrostics involve word play.

FOR OLDER STUDENTS

Encourage the use of double acrostics and poems with phrases or sentences rather than single words.

EVERYDAY PARALLELS

Completing a crossword puzzle or playing a game of Scrabble are both related to the mind games involved in writing acrostics. The television game, "Wheel of Fortune," uses many of the same thinking skills.

WHAT THIS FORM OFFERS

- The acrostic introduces a conventional poetry form.
- It encourages word play.
- The acrostic opens up opportunities to use new vocabulary.
- It gives logical thinkers a door into poetry writing.
- It can be as adventurous as the poet wants it to be.

ACROSTIC

ROSE

Raspberry red
Opening slowly
Sweet-sniffing
Elegant

BAGEL

Butter
All over
Gobble
Every
Last crumb

ACROSTIC

CROW

Cawing
Raucous
indigO
    Winging

SNAKE

Slithering scales

Nimbly navigating,

Armless and adorned like

Knights in armor,

Electrically energetic!

SMOOTHIE

Slurpable

Mush

Offering

Overwhelmingly

Thirst-quenching

Hunger-quashing

Infinite

Energy

DOUBLE ACROSTIC

Money Blues

My money tends to flow, but mostly eb**b**.

Occasionally I have Jackson's face on a bil**l**.

Naturally, I tend to compare to someone with all the electronic toys, like Y-O-**U**.

Eventually, but not today, maybe it'll sink in that money is nic**e**,

Yet, get real! It isn't some magic wand that'll—kabam—erase all my issue**s**.

Think-through: My thoughts while writing "Snake," "Smoothie" and "Money Blues"

First Thoughts

Before I start, I want to take a minute to think about the kinds of acrostics I'd like to write. There are many different ways to write them, from very simple to quite complex.

- I'll have one acrostic made up of a series of phrases or words.
- I'll have another acrostic that reads like a complete sentence.
- I'll try one that's a double acrostic where the first and last letters of every line form words.

Getting Started

While I'm on my walk I'll brainstorm some interesting words—animals, food, and other miscellany. Here are some of the words I jotted down: snake, bagel, rose, spider, money, garden, school, robin, crow, ice cream, yogurt, smoothie. I'll think about the letters in some of these words and see if they inspire me, if they have potential.

First Draft

I'll take another walk and jot down ideas for the letters of some of the words. For some reason, walking helps me with this form.

Here's an acrostic with one word for each letter of the word "snake" and another using the word "smoothie."

SNAKE

Slithering
Nimble
Armless
Knightly
Electric

SMOOTHIE

Slurpable
Mush
Offering
Overwhelmingly
Thirst-quenching
Hunger-quashing
Infinite
Energy

For the following acrostic, I thought of the title while on a walk, but I had to sit down and map it out in order to write the first draft. I wrote the letters of the words money blues and started filling in some possible phrases that started and ended with the correct letters.

M	b
O	l
N	u
E	e
Y	s

Money Blues

My money tends to flow and eb**b**.
Occasionally I have a twenty-dollar bil**l**
Naturally, I tend to compare to yo**u**.
Eventually, I'll learn that money is nic**e**,
Yet it doesn't magically dissolve all problem**s**.

Revising/Experimenting

The snake acrostic is too simple. I'm going to use some alliteration to make it more interesting. I want each line to glide into the next like the movements of a snake.

SNAKE

Slithering scales
Nimbly navigating,
Armless and adorned like
Knights in armor,
Electrically energetic!

The smoothie poem came out well. I'll keep it.

I need to make "Money Blues" more of a poem—less direct. I'll show what I mean with an image instead of telling the information directly. For example, I'll talk about Jackson's face instead of saying a $20 bill.

I'll put in some figurative language by comparing money to a magic wand.

Right now the ending falls flat so I'll work on the rhythm in the last lines.

Money Blues

My money tends to flow, and often eb**b**.

Occasionally I have Jackson's face on a bi**ll**.

Naturally, I tend to compare to someone with all the electronic toys, like yo**u**.

Eventually—but not today—maybe it'll sink in that money is nic**e**,

Yet it is no magic wand with stars shooting out the end that solves all problem**s**.

I'll get a little edgier in the last line and add a sound.

Yet, get real, it's no magic wand that'll—kabam—erase all my issue**s**.

Final Draft

See pages 58-60.

Notes on Poems

ROSE: Notice the alliteration of the r-words (*raspberry red*) and the s-words (*sweet-sniffing*). There is assonance, where the vowel sounds in several words are the same. In this case, it's the *o* sound in "opening slowly."

BAGEL: I wanted the acrostic to flow, rather than being completely disjointed words.

CROW: The acrostic is unusual because the *O* comes from the end of the word "indigo" instead of the beginning. This made the poem look a little bit like a bird in flight.

See Think-through for "Snake," "Smoothie" and "Money Blues."

BIBLIOGRAPHY: ACROSTIC

ELEMENTARY SCHOOL

Anonymous. "Does Only Good . . . ," *A Kick in the Head.* Cambridge: Candlewick Press, 2005, p. 36.

Fisher, Aileen. "All in a Word," *Side by Side, Poems to Read Together* collected by Lee Bennett Hopkins. New York: Simon & Schuster, 1988, p. 28.

Franco, Betsy. "One," *Counting Our Way to the 100th Day!* New York: Margaret K. McElderry Books, 2004, p. 15.

Janeczko, Paul B. "Can't Avoid Trouble . . . ," *A Kick in the Head.* Cambridge: Candlewick Press, 2005, p. 36.

Lansky, Bruce. *How to Write Acrostic Poems.* Retrieved October 5, 2004 from **http://www.poetryteachers.com/poetclass/lessons/acrostic.html.**

Paolilli, Paul and Dan Brewer. *Silver Seeds.* New York: Viking, 2001.

Schnur, Steven. *Autumn: An Alphabet Acrostic.* New York: Clarion Books, 1997.

Schnur, Steven. *Spring: An Alphabet Acrostic.* New York: Clarion Books, 1999.

Schnur, Steven. *Summer: An Alphabet Acrostic.* New York: Clarion Books, 2001.

Schnur, Steven. *Winter: An Alphabet Acrostic*. New York: Clarion Books, 2002.

MIDDLE SCHOOL AND HIGH SCHOOL

Carroll, Lewis. "A boat, beneath a sunny sky. . ." *Through the Looking Glass*. [last poem in the book is an acrostic for the name "Alice Pleasance Liddell" who was the inspiration for the book]

Lewis, J. Patrick. "Necessary Gardens," *Please Bury Me in the Library*. New York: Harcourt, 2005.

Lewis, J. Patrick. "Notes From a Day in the Bush," *Vherses: Poems for Outstanding Women*. Mankato, Minnesota: Creative Editions, 2005.

13 BALLAD
Recommended for Grades 4-12

BACKGROUND

The ballad is a story told in poetry that comes from the storytelling tradition of the folk song. Scholars disagree about whether early ballads were written by single poets or were written communally. Though there are ballads from all countries and all cultures, some sources say that the earliest ballads in English were composed hundreds of years ago in the geographical area between England and Scotland. In this untamed countryside, clan rivalries abounded and stories about ghosts and fairies were popular. The ballad was perfect for the storytellers at the time, because this form involves telling dramatic, tragic, and/or supernatural tales. In the 1700s, poets began writing ballads without music, but the poems continued to have a strong song-like quality.

CHARACTERISTICS OF A BALLAD

- The ballad tells a story with a strong plot.
- The story is stripped down, and there is little character development. The story is mostly action, which at times, is so streamlined, the reader has to study the poem to determine the plot.
- The story is about a specific dramatic event. Sometimes it chronicles an historical event or a legendary person from history, either heroic or villainous.
- The plot focuses on the conflict or problem. Typically, it stresses the dark side of a story, frequently concerning love lost, death, violence, tragedy, or the supernatural.
- The poem creates an immediate feeling, as if you're there, and the emotions are strong.
- It often paints rich, haunting images in the reader's mind.
- The rhyme scheme of the ballad is often ABCB. It can also be ABAB. (See *rhyme scheme* in Glossary.)
- The ballad is usually written in four-line stanzas (quatrains).

- The first and third lines typically have 4 beats and the second and third have 3. (See *beat* in Glossary.)

    da DA, da DA, da DA, da DA (called iambic tetrameter)

    da DA, da DA, da DA (called iambic trimeter)

- A phrase or refrain is often repeated throughout.

EVERYDAY PARALLELS

Stories that people tell when "shooting the breeze," at campfires or at other gatherings, are like ballads. Folk singers and country western singers often sing ballads that tell a poignant story. Popular music on the radio sometimes tells a story about love or loss. Newscasters often tell tragic stories on the news.

WHAT THIS FORM OFFERS

- The ballad introduces a conventional poetry form.
- The rhythm is natural and easy to write.
- Ballads give students a chance to use rhyme effectively.
- They offer an opportunity to tell a story, possibly a personal one, in a poem.
- They give students a chance to learn how to develop a strong plot and keep the action moving.
- This form gives students a chance to read old, traditional ballads.

BALLAD

Ballad of the Basement Band

They began in Joey's basement.
where they improvised and jammed.
Danika had the coolest voice.
She said, "We've got a band!"
Danika, with the coolest pipes, said,
"Guys, we've got a band."

They pooled their cash and bought
equipment—all of it was used.
Created a sound to suit them all,
part folksong and part blues.
Came up with a sound to please them all,
part folksong and part blues.

They played for friends and family,
even got some real gigs.
Then Danika won a contest
and she started getting big.
Yes, Danika came out number one,
began to make it big.

They begged Danika, "Stay with us.
You're vital to our group!
Don't forget your modest start.
Don't forget your roots.
Don't forget we helped you start.
Don't ignore your roots."

"I'm loyal," Danika said to them.
"I'll always be true blue.
But agents, fame are calling me.
I'm not sure what to do.
The call of fame is pulling me.
It's not clear what to do."

Emotions revved to fever pitch.
and envy built and soared.
"You're arrogant, big-headed,"
the three band members roared.
"You've got a royal attitude!"
They shouted and they roared.

Danika finally pulled away,
the others split apart,
all clinging to bittersweet memories
of their basement-jammin' start,
all clinging to bittersweet memories
of their basement-jammin' start.

Think-through: My thoughts while writing "Ballad of the Basement Band"

First Thoughts

I could write about the raccoon who came in the cat door of someone's house. It makes me think of the Beatles' "Rocky Raccoon" song.

Or I could write about some figure in history, such as Ned Kelly in Australia or a Native American chief.

Or I could use a story I once wrote about a band. The story ended happily but I could have the band break up at the end of my ballad.

Getting Started

I like the band idea because lots of kids would like to be in bands.

The whole idea of a band goes with the tone of a ballad because being in a band has its ups and downs, and often bands break up.

Things can get dramatic, too.

I'll use stories I've heard about bands starting in people's basements.

I can also use stories my famous friend has told me about starting several bands and what happened.

Third Draft

I included my third draft below, instead of my first draft, because I wanted to focus on the changes I made to this third draft:

The Band

They began in Joey's basement.
where bare light bulbs sputtered and glared.
They added guitars and a drum set
to the laundry and crates down there.

They sounded pretty good that day.
as they improvised and jammed.
Danika had the coolest voice.
She said, "We've got a band!"

They pooled whatever cash they had,
for equipment, borrowed and used,
created a sound to suit them all,
part folksong and part blues.

They played for friends and family,
even got some real gigs.
Then Danika won a contest
and she started getting big.

Danika sometimes sang with them, or At first her fame excited them
her oldest, closest fans.
But jealousy took over
and affected the whole band.

Danika finally pulled away,
the others split apart,
all clinging to bittersweet memories
of their basement-jammin' start.

Revising/Experimenting

Some background: In my first draft I said they played down in the basement
with lots of junk around them and then I made the junk more specific. I had
several drafts in which the band split apart because they went to different high
schools. Then I made Danika win a contest and that worked a lot better. I had
drafts in which I told what happened to each person in the band at the end.
But I made it more emotional by saying that they split apart and kept their bittersweet memories of their basement start. I changed it to "basement jammin'
start" for the sound of it.

Now I need to revise draft 3. When I read it to Maria Damon who is a poet and
professor of poetry, she made suggestions. In response to her ideas, I made some
decisions:

- I'd better combine the first two stanzas to get right into the action.

    They began in Joey's basement.
    where they improvised and jammed.
    Danika had the coolest voice.
    She said, "We've got a band!"

- I'll heighten the drama by revving up the emotions in the poem and by
  heightening the conflict. I'll make it feel more immediate by including
  conversation.

    "I'm loyal to them." Danika said.
    "I'll always be true blue.
    But agents, fame are calling me.
    I'm not sure what to do."

    Emotions revved to fever pitch.
    and envy built and soared.
    "You think you're so much better than us!"
    the three band members roared.

- I'll add some repetition to each stanza to make it sound more ballad-like.
  In fact, I'll repeat the last two lines of each stanza, with some variation.

    They began in Joey's basement.
    where they improvised and jammed.
    Danika had the coolest voice.

69

She said, "We've got a band!"
Danika, with the coolest pipes, said,
"Guys, we've got a band."

They pooled whatever cash they had,
for equipment—mostly used,
created a sound to suit them all,
part folksong and part blues.
Came up with a sound to please them all,
part folksong and part blues.

Final Draft

See page 67.

BIBLIOGRAPHY: BALLAD

ELEMENTARY

Anonymous. "The Mouse, the Frog, and the Little Red Hen," *Side by Side, Poems to Read Together* collected by Lee Bennett Hopkins. New York: Simon & Schuster, 1988, p. 50-51.

Lewis, J. Patrick. *Tulip at the Bat.* New York: Little, Brown and Company, 2006.

McNaughton, Colin. "Frankenstein's Monster is Finally Dead!" "The Crocodile with Toothache," *Making Friends with Frankenstein.* Cambridge: Candlewick Press, 1994, p. 24-25, 72-73.

Silverstein, Shel. "Jimmy Jet and His TV Set," *Where the Sidewalk Ends.* New York, Harper & Row, 1974, p. 28-29.

ALL LEVELS

Anonymous. "The Fox," *Poem-Making* by Myra Cohn Livingston. New York: HarperCollins, 1991, pp. 50-51.

Carroll, Lewis. "Jabberwocky," *The Random House Book of Poetry*, selected by Jack Prelutsky. New York: Random House, 1983, p. 170.

Longfellow, Henry Wadsworth. "Paul Revere's Ride," *Once Upon a Poem.* New York: The Chicken House, Scholastic, 2004, p. 18-25.

Longfellow, Henry Wadsworth. *The Midnight Ride of Paul Revere.* Brooklyn, New York: Handprint Books, 2001.

Noyes, Alfred. "The Highwayman," *Once Upon a Poem.* New York: The Chicken House, Scholastic, 2004, p. 69-77.

Paterson, A.B. "Banjo," "The Man from Snowy River," *Once Upon a Poem.* New York: The Chicken House, Scholastic, 2004, p. 40-47.

Service, Robert W. "The Cremation of Sam McGee," *Once Upon a Poem.* New York: The Chicken House, Scholastic, 2004, p. 94-101.

Service, Robert W. Selection from "The Shooting of Dan McGrew," *A Kick in the Head,* selected by Paul B. Janeczko. Cambridge: Candlewick Press, 2005, pp. 48-49.

Thayer, Ernest Lawrence. *Casey at the Bat: A Ballad of the Republic Sung in 1888.* Brooklyn, New York: Handprint Books, 2000.

Wilson, Raymond. "The Grateful Dragon," *Once Upon a Poem.* New York: The Chicken House, Scholastic, 2004, p. 62-68.

MIDDLE SCHOOL AND HIGH SCHOOL

Coleridge, Samuel Taylor. "Rime of the Ancient Mariner," *Wonko '04.* Retrieved on October 1, 2004 from **http://www.wonko.info/albatross/default.htm#PART1.**

Hughes, Langston. "Ballad of the Miser" *The Collected Poems of Langston Hughes.* New York: Vintage Books, 1994, pp. 221.

Koertge, Ron. "After the Funeral," *Shakespeare Bats Cleanup.* Cambridge: Candlewick Press, 2003, p. 37-38.

Laidlaw, Brian. "Empty-Handed, " "Twenty," *Quarter-Life, Poems and Music,* 2004, pp. 28, 29. See **www.brianlaidlaw.com.**

Longfellow, Henry Wadsworth. "The Wreck of the Hesperus," *A Blupete Poetry Pick,* selected by Peter Landry. Retrieved October 4, 2004 from

http://www.blupete.com/Literature/Poetry/Wreck.htm.

Poe, Edgar Allan. "Annabel Lee," *A Little Archive of Poetry.* Retrieved August 13, 2005 from **http://www.poeticportal.net/NOPQ_/poe-edgar.html.**

Service, Robert W. "The Shooting of Dan McGrew," *A Blupete Poetry Pick,* selected by Peter Landry. Retrieved October 4, 2004 from **http://www.blupete.com/Literature/Poetry/ServiceShooting.htm.**

The Beatles. "Rocky Raccoon." Retrieved October 8, 2004 from **http://www.elyrics.net/go/b/beatles-lyrics/rocky-raccoon-lyrics/.**

Traditional. "The Ballad of Barbara Allen," prepared by Avi Tsur. Retrieved October 4, 2004 from **http://www.etni.org.il/music/barbaraallen.htm.**

14 BLUES POEM
Recommended for Grades K-12

BACKGROUND

Blues music originated sometime during the era of slavery; therefore, some of its roots are African. The slaves sang songs called "work songs" or "field hollers." This oral tradition developed into many forms of music, including gospel, the blues (sung by people such as Bessie Smith and Billie Holiday), jazz, rhythm and blues, and even military drill songs. The poet Langston Hughes was a major figure in transforming blues music into a written form of poetry. The blues poem traditionally deals with the downside of life—depression, despair, tragedy, suffering, loss. But there is a hopeful aspect to these poems, a strong spirit to them.

CHARACTERISTICS OF A BLUES POEM

- The blues poem is a poem of complaint, despair, tragedy, loss, struggle.
- It usually involves repetition. Traditionally, the first line is repeated in the second line, exactly the same or with some variation. These two lines are followed by a third line that rhymes with the first two. There can be many stanza, or verses, like this.
- Each of the three lines in each stanza is usually broken into two lines so the stanza is actually six lines long.
- The poem describes a situation rather than telling a story.
- The poet gets into the depths of a problem, but underlying the words is a feeling of hopefulness and a sense of the poet's undying spirit.
- The poet is healing his or her despair by expressing it in the poem.
- Sometimes the uplifting part of the poem is the humor subtly interwoven into the poem, but the general tone is serious.
- Some blues poems do not have the element of repetition. This free form version of blues poetry can be identified by the subject matter and tone.
- Blues poems don't have to rhyme but they often do. The rhyme is often slant-rhyme where the words almost rhyme, such as *lawn* and *strong* or *leave* and *live*.
- Language can be informal and/or written in a dialect.

EVERYDAY PARALLELS

The everyday complaining and whining people do is akin to the blues, particularly if a sense of humor is interwoven. Of course, blues music is the root of the blues poem. When friends say they're having a bad day, or are feeling depressed, and they reel off the bad situations they've been going through, they are close to composing a blues poem.

WHAT THIS FORM OFFERS

- The blues poem introduces a conventional poetry form.
- It teaches students about a period of history in music and poetry.
- It teaches about a form that is important in African-American history.
- Students learn to use repetition, a tool they can use when writing other types of poetry.
- The blues poem provides an opportunity for students to air their grievances and complaints.
- It offers a chance for students to recognize that everyone has a shadow side, that everyone has feelings of loss, grief, despair, frustration, but that there's a way to get through it. Through blues poetry, students can learn that one of the first steps out of a problem is expressing it and possibly seeing it with a hint of humor or irony.

BLUES POEM

Recess Blues

Feelin' sick at school today.
Feelin' sick at school today.
Can't do my work
and I can't even play.

In the office, waitin' for dad.
In the office, waitin' for dad.
Why'd I pick recess
to feel so bad?

BLUES POEM

Hole in My Pocket

I biked to the store
with the money I'd saved.
I biked to the store
with the money I'd saved.
The neighbors got
a smile and a wave.

Had a hole in my pocket—
no money at all.
Had a hole in my pocket—
no money at all.
I couldn't buy
that basketball!

BLUES POEM

House Chore Blues

Gotta take the garbage out.
Rancid, stinkin' stuff.
Gotta carry garbage out.
Heavy, rancid stuff.
Ants all over the outdoor cans!
Heck, I've had enough.

Gotta clean my bedroom up.
Can barely see the floor.
Gotta straighten up my room.
Can hardly open the door.
Never gonna finish chores—
They pile on more and more.

Can't leave home till Dad inspects.
Pals are waitin' for me.
Can't leave home till chores are done.
Pals are honkin' for me.
Just wait till I am on my own.
Then I'll be free. Home-free.

Think-through: My thoughts while writing "House Chore Blues"

First Thoughts

I could write a heavy poem about parents arguing and a kid hearing it every night, or about a kid getting caught shoplifting, or about being injured in a sport and not being able to play in the big game.

But I think I'll stick to something less heavy because when I write about heavy things, I tend to get too dark.

Maybe some of the students will write about the darker things. That would be good. And I've included two weighty poems in the read-throughs on pages xx-xx and more in the bibliography, particularly in the teen anthologies I compiled. (See "You Hear Me?," "Things I have to tell you," and "Night is Gone, Day is Still Coming" in the bibliographies for free verse, list poem, ode, persona poem, and sonnet.)

I'll write about a twisted ankle or a kid who has to finish chores she put off before going out with friends. When that happened to my kids, they hated it.

Getting Started

I'll do the house chore blues idea.

I'll start writing and see if the rhymes or off-rhymes work.

I'll write about taking out the garbage and cleaning up a room and maybe doing laundry.

No, just the first two ideas.

First Draft

> Gotta take the garbage out.
> Rancid, stinkin' stuff.
> Gotta take the garbage out.
> Rancid, stinkin' stuff.
> We've got two giant garbage cans,
> as if one isn't enough.
>
> Gotta clean up my room.
> Can barely see the floor.
> Gotta clean up my room.
> Dirty clothes all over the floor.
> Never gonna finish
> There's more and more and more. OR what a tug of war. OR what a bore.
>
> Can't go out till chores are done.
> Katie's waiting for me.
> Can't go out till dad inspects.
> Down the block she'll be.
> Can't wait till I'm grown up.
> How messy I'll let myself be.

78

Can't wait till I'm all grown up
Whoo, how messy I will be.

Think of how messy I'll let myself be!

Revising/Experimenting

Now I'm going to revise.
I'll make a variation in the first stanza. Langston Hughes often varies the repetitive lines a little.

> Gotta take the garbage out.
> Rancid, stinkin' stuff.
> Gotta take the garbage out.
> Heavy, stinkin' stuff.

What I said about two garbage cans doesn't make sense, so I'll think of something else gross about the job.

> Ants all over the outdoor cans,
> as if it weren't enough OR I've really had enough OR
> Heck, I've had enough.

The rhythm in the second stanza is off. I'll rhyme "floor" and "door" even though the second and fourth lines usually end with the same word. I noticed Langston Hughes did this in one poem.

> Gotta clean my bedroom up.
> Can barely see the floor.
> Gotta straighten up my room.
> Can hardly open the door.
> Never gonna finish chores—
> They pile on more and more.

I'll make it more general in the last stanza and change the ending to be angrier.

> Can't leave the house till Dad inspects.
> Pals waitin' outside for me.
> Can't leave the house till chores are done.
> Pals honkin' out there for me.
> Just wait till I am on my own.
> Then I'll be free. Home free.

I like that "home-free" usually means safe, but here it means free of all the chores and nagging that goes with living at home.

79

Final Draft

See page 77.

Notes on poems

Recess Blues: This poem has the traditional repetition of a blues poem but an elementary school student can relate to it, even a kindergartner.

Hole in My Pocket: I waited until the last line to clear up what the kid wanted to buy, to give it more weight.

House Chore Blues: See Think-through.

Note: The acrostic, "Money Blues," on page 60 could also be a blues poem.

BIBLIOGRAPHY: BLUES POEM

ELEMENTARY SCHOOL

Frame, Jeron Ashford. *Yesterday I Had the Blues*. Berkeley: Tricycle Press, 2003.

Greenfield, Eloise. "Little Boy Blues," *Night on Neighborhood Street*. New York: Dial Books for Young Readers, 1991.

Greenfield, Eloise. "Things," *Honey, I Love*. New York: HarperTrophy, 1978.

Heide, Florence Parry. "Grounded," *The 20th Century Children's Poetry Treasury*, selected by Jack Prelutsky. New York: Alfred A. Knopf, 1999, p. 40.

Hughes, Langston. "Mother to Son," "Poem," *Tomie dePaola's Book of Poems*, edited by Tomie dePaola. New York: G.P. Putnam's Sons, 1988, p. 55, 56.

Katz, Bobbi. "Back-to-School Blues," *A Kick in the Head*, selected by Paul B. Janeczko. Cambridge: Candlewick Press, 2005, p. 50.

Kirk, Daniel. "dog-bone blues," "Howlin' Time," *Dogs Rule*. New York: Hyperion, 2003, p. 30-31, 43.

Prelutsky, Jack. "I Should Have Stayed in Bed Today," *Something Big Has Been Here*. New York: Greenwillow, 1990, p. 28-29.

Viorst, Judith. "Since Hanna Moved Away," *The Random House Book of Poetry*, selected by Jack Prelutsky. New York: Random House, 1983, p. 114.

MIDDLE SCHOOL AND HIGH SCHOOL

Blues songs sung by Bessie Smith, Robert Johnson, Billie Holiday.

Hughes, Langston. "Mother to Son," "Homesick Blues," "Bound No'th Blues," "Lonesome Place," "Tired," "Out of Work," *The Collected Poems of Langston Hughes*. New York: Vintage Books, 1994, pp. 30, 72, 76, 135, 217.

Lewis, J. Patrick. "Movin' Out Movin' On Blues," *Black Cat Bone: A Life of Delta Blues Legend Robert Johnson*. Mankato, Minnesota: Creative Editions, 2006.

Mann, Becky. "Contemplating fat and thin . . .," *Things I Have to Tell You, poems and writing by teenage girls*. Cambridge: Candlewick Press, 2001, 21.

Myers, Walter Dean. *Blues Journey.* New York: Holiday House, 2003.

Young, Kevin, edited by. *Blues Poems.* New York: Everyman's Library, 2003.

15 DIAMANTE AND CINQUAIN

Recommended for Grades K-12

BACKGROUND

The diamanté and the cinquain are grouped together because they were both created in the early 1900s by an American poet and English teacher, Adelaide Crapsey, who died very young. In French, the name *diamanté* means *diamond* for the diamond shape of the poem, and *cinquain* means *five* for the number of lines in the poem. Crapsey was influenced by the Japanese form of poetry called haiku; her forms are also short and have strict rules about their structure. The diamanté is appropriate for primary poets and the cinquain for older poets.

CHARACTERISTICS OF A DIAMANTE

- The diamanté is formally a 7-line poem, but many classroom teachers also use it successfully as a 5-line poem.
- Strictly speaking, in the 7-line form, the first word is the opposite of the last word.

Line 1: 1 noun that is the subject
Line 2: 2 adjectives that describe the noun
Line 3: 3 verbs ending in *-ing* that describe the noun
Line 4: 4 nouns: the first two refer to line 1, the second two refer to line 7
Line 5: 3 verbs ending in *-ing* that describe line 7
Line 6: 2 adjectives that describe line 7
Line 7: 1 noun that is the opposite of line 1

The 5- line form is more like this:
Line 1: 1 noun that is the subject
Line 2: 2 adjectives that describe the noun
Line 3: 3 verbs ending in *-ing* that describe the noun
Line 4: your feelings about the noun
Line 5: another name for the noun

As poet Joy Hulme suggests, the slightly disjointed words that make up the lines of the diamanté can be combined and smoothed into cohesive phrases for a more satisfying poem. (See my samples about the bee and the egg.)

CHARACTERISTICS OF THE CINQUAIN

- The cinquain follows a formula, although even Crapsey deviated at times.
Line 1: the subject or title, 2 syllables

Line 2: 4 syllables
Line 3: 6 syllables
Line 4: 8 syllables
Line 5: 2 syllables

- The poem flows from one line to the next, rather than stopping to pause at the end of each line.
- The poem is usually one thought, feeling, or reflection.
- There's a feeling of movement, as if a thought is unraveling, as if a subtle change is taking place from the beginning of the poem to the end.
- The last line is often somewhat surprising.
- The syllables in the first and last lines are often strongly stressed syllables, such as in the words *moonlight* and *sea foam*.

EVERYDAY PARALLELS

Greeting cards sometimes have a short unrhymed phrase that is somewhat contemplative. The journal of someone out in nature might resemble a cinquain. On a walk, a person might notice a scene in nature or an interaction between people and think about it afterwards. These thoughts are like a cinquain.

WHAT THESE FORMS OFFER

- These forms introduce conventional poetry forms.
- They challenge students to follow formulas regarding numbers of words or syllables, linking poetry to mathematical thinking. Note that the restrictions can be loosened.
- The diamanté offers a reinforcement of parts of speech.
- The 7-line diamanté allows students to think about opposites, transformations, antonyms.
- The cinquain provides an opportunity to develop a single subject in a subtle but moving way.
- The cinquain elicits short powerful poetry by restricting syllables in each line.

DIAMANTE

bumblebees
fuzzy, busy, buzzy
working, cooperating, honeying
I wish bees didn't sting.
buzzers

or

bumblebees
fuzzy, busy, buzzy
cooperative honey-makers
Too bad bees sting!
buzzers

DIAMANTE

egg
oval, infinite
holding, waiting, protecting
whiteness, hardness, yellowness, softness
cracking, struggling, peeking
fluffy, wobbly
chick

or

egg
oval, infinite
protective covering
white, hard, yellow, soft
struggling to get out
fluffy, wobbly
chick

CINQUAINS

Moist snail.
what strange message
did you leave on the ground
as a journal of your nighttime
raiding?

Breathing,
like paper trash
in an unexpected wind storm,
can seem more like the moon than a
cat's eye.

Moonlight
spreading slowly
through my curtainless room,
limbering my active mind for
dreaming.

Think-through: My thoughts while writing the cinquain about moonlight

First Thoughts

I need a topic that goes from point A to point B and involves some movement or change.

I could write about a snail, some trash in the wind, moonlight coming in the window, fall leaves, loneliness.

I've written about moonlight before, but there's lots of room for another poem about moonlight.

Getting Started

I can see the moonlight coming in my bedroom window at night—it's very subtle. Actually, if I'm honest about this, I don't see the moonlight coming in, I usually see moon shadows on the lawn when I get up in the middle of the night.

I'm going to pretend there are distinct moonbeams coming in the room anyway.

It's a mysterious time of night when I'm just falling asleep.

I'll just start writing with the syllable count of 2, 3, 6, 8, 2 (the syllables for a cinquain) and see what happens.

I'll start with a noun, *moonlight.*

First Draft

My first draft:

> Moonlight
> spreading slowly
> through my room without curtains,
> setting a stage of soft shadows,
> for sleep.

Revising/Experimenting

Now I'm going to revise.

I like the first three lines but the third line has too many syllables. I'll change it to:

> through my curtainless room.

The ending isn't as powerful as I want it to be.
Maybe it's the words "shadows" and "sleep." They sort of put me to sleep.

Really what's happening when I'm falling asleep is my mind is slowing down. I'll write about that.

> loosening my active mind for
> sleeping.

I still don't think the word "sleeping" is very surprising and doesn't bring up any picture in my mind. The last line of the cinquain is supposed to be a surprise or at least a little unexpected. I'll try something different.

> loosening my active mind for
> dreaming.

That works. It has more movement toward an unexpected ending, and the word "dreaming" is much richer than "sleeping."

I'll change "loosening" to "limbering." That's closer to what I mean.

> Moonlight
> spreading slowly
> through my curtainless room,
> limbering my active mind for
> dreaming.

Let's get real. I'm obsessed with thoughts as I'm going off to sleep and can't let them go.

> substitutes my obsessive thoughts
> with dreams.

I like this because dreams has a double meaning, but it isn't fun to say. Here's another try that sounds better and is closer to what really goes on.

> tranquilizing my crazy mind for
> dreaming.

I think I'll go back to what I had. It flows. But it was good to experiment with other ideas.

> limbering my active mind for
> dreaming.

Final Draft

See page 87.

Notes on Poems

Diamanté: For the bee and egg poems, I did one traditional diamanté, and then I used Joy Hulme's suggestion to smooth out the lines. That's why there are two versions.

Cinquain: "Moist snails": The word "raiding" used to be "travels," but that wasn't a surprising word. Snails raid the garden at night, eating the leaves.

Breathing: I was reading an article about letting your mind loose and letting images come from around you and not from such a logical place when writing poetry. I was having fun and just thinking about images and sounds in this poem. I could see the moon, my cat was climbing on me, and I had some trash next to me to throw away.

Moonlight: See Think-through on pages 88-89.

BIBLIOGRAPHY: DIAMANTE AND CINQUAIN

ELEMENTARY SCHOOL

[Some of the poems below are cinquains and diamantés and some are five-line poems that are close to cinquains.]

Alarcón, Francisco X. "Spring," *Laughing Tomatoes.* San Francisco: Children's Book Press, 1997, p. 11.

Aldis, Dorothy. "When I Was Lost," *The 20th Century Children's Poetry Treasury*, selected by Jack Prelutsky. New York: Alfred A. Knopf, 1999, p. 65.

George, Kristine O'Connell. "Sketchbook on Easel," *Old Elm Speaks.* New York: Clarion, 1998, p. 28.

Giovanni, Nikki. "fear," "the boy in the barber shop," "the drum," *Spin a Soft Black Song.* New York: HarperCollins, 1987, pp. 18, 35, 41.

Lewis, J. Patrick. "Oh Calendar!" *The Family Read-Aloud Holiday Treasury,* compiled by Alice Low. New York: Little, Brown and Company, 1991.

Livingston, Myra Cohn. "Labor Day," "Thanksgiving," *Celebrations.* New York: Holiday House, 1985, p. 23, 29.

Morrison, Lillian. "Rain Sound," *The 20th Century Children's Poetry Treasury,* selected by Jack Prelutsky. New York: Alfred A. Knopf, 1999, p. 29.

ALL LEVELS

Janeczko, Paul B. "Oh, cat . . . ," *A Kick in the Head,* selected by Paul B. Janeczko. Cambridge: Candlewick Press, 2005, p. 18.

Livingston, Myra Cohn. "T-shirt," *Class 324, Poetry,* The Cinquain menu. Retrieved October 1, 2004 from **http://www.cqsb.qc.ca/svs/434/tpoetry.htm.**

MIDDLE SCHOOL AND HIGH SCHOOL

Cinquain. Retrieved September 28, 2004 from **http://www.ahapoetry.com/cinqhmpg.htm.**

Crapsey, Adelaide. *Bob's Byway: Adelaide Crapsey.* Retrieved September 28, 2004 from **http://www.poeticbyway.com/xcrapsey.htm.**

Crapsey, Adelaide. "Triad, " "The Warning," *Modern American Poetry,* edited by Louis Untermeyer. Retrieved September 28, 2004 from **http://www.bartleby.com/104/index2.html.**

16 FOUND POEM
Recommended for Grades 4-12

BACKGROUND

Strictly speaking, to create a found poem, the poet takes part of a non-poetic piece of text, such as a news article, an informal note, or a list, and reformats it into lines and stanzas to make it a poem. Even an overheard conversation will work. There are examples of this form in the early 1900s in which train schedules or travel books were used to create a poem. Surrealist poets enjoyed this form. So did Ezra Pound, whose poems included letters written by Jefferson and Adams, among other things. In this age of the Internet, there is a web site that posts found poems that people have sent in from around the world. (See *Found Magazine* in Bibliography on page 100.)

Sometimes poets take liberties with the found poem, making a collage of found phrases from different sources, such as magazines, cereal boxes, and advertisements.

Some people consider William Carlos Williams' famous poem, "This Is Just to Say," a faux, or fake, found poem because it sounds like a note he left on the kitchen table after eating all the plums in the icebox. No one knows if Williams really left the note or made it up, but his poem gives you an idea of the nature of a found poem. (See Bibliography on page 100.)

CHARACTERISTICS OF A FOUND POEM

- The found poem uses a part of a text or conversation that is not a poem and reformats it to create a poem.
- The poet gives the piece a title, breaks up the lines, and decides how much of the text to use.
- The poet uses such sources as news articles, sticky notes, lists, or overheard conversations.
- The text that is used has some unexpected poetic feeling to it once it is reformatted.
- The less the poet does to the found poem, the better.
- Sometimes the poet gathers phrases from different sources and creates a collage that becomes a poem.

EVERYDAY PARALLELS

In the course of a day, people often run across a part of a news article, a note passed in class, a sticky note on the refrigerator, a birthday list, a conversation, or a sign that seems poetic even though it's not supposed to be a poem.

WHAT THIS FORM OFFERS

- Found poetry introduces a conventional poetry form.
- Students learn the power of the line break—how and where the poet decides to break the poem into lines. (How short are the lines? Where does the poet end one line and begin another?)
- Students begin to see poetry everywhere.
- Found poetry makes them more alert to text in their environment.
- It challenges students' conception of what constitutes poetry.
- It teaches them a form of poetry that is somewhat surrealistic, as opposed to some of the classical styles they are accustomed to.
- Interesting juxtapositions in found poetry can help the mind go places it hasn't been before.
- Found poetry broadens vocabulary.
- It introduces students to the freedom and joy of playing with language.

FOUND POEM

**Note on Jake the Snake's Cage
on Tuesday at 9:00 a.m.**

Please don't tap or knock on
Jake's cage for the next 24 hours.
Jake gets jumpy after I feed him
a mouse.

FOUND POEM

Stormy

If some offensive
words escaped my
lips, let the storm-
winds blow them
hence. Just like cats'
teeth need special
care, the lamp of
fame casts a
fickle glow.

FOUND POEM

poetic sign language

EVERYBODY KNOWS:

if you don't

Stand up and shout.

GRAVITY SAYS YOU

Will Never Be
The Same.™

Go fish

FOUND POEM

Which Way
Is Up?

Inside the Moon

Stealaway

Please Hurry!

Think-through: My thoughts while writing the found poems

First Thoughts

I'm going to write different kinds of found poems.

Note poem: I'll write one where I take a note I've found on the sidewalk or in a classroom. I'll make the note into a poem. Or I'll use something someone has said recently. Or I could use that stub I got at a parking lot, for my windshield, that said I could park there until 2041!

Found poem from 3 sources: I'll gather a phrase from 3 different sources, such as a newspaper, a food can, and a book. I'll arrange them in a way that's intriguing.

Collage found poem: I'll cut phrases from magazines or newspapers and put them together to form a collage/found poem. (See pages 95 and 96.)

Getting Started

Poem 1: One of the teachers I visited left a note for the maintenance people who were fixing the lights in her room. It was about not bothering the snake after it had been fed. Good topic.

Poem 2: I'll gather a quote from *The Odyssey*, from the sign I saw on the Dempster Dumpster, and from the newspaper.

Poem 3: I'll cut phrases from magazines and rearrange them until they form an interesting poem.

First Draft

Poem 1:
Note on Jake the Snake's Cage on Tuesday at 9:00 a.m.

> Please don't tap or knock on Jake's cage
> for the next 24 hours.
> Jake gets jumpy after I feed him a mouse.

Poem 2:

> **Stormy**
>
> If some offensive
> words escaped my
> lips, let the storm-
> winds blow them
> hence. Not for
> rubbish, the lamp of
> fame casts a
> fickle glow.

[got phrases from: *The Odyssey*, Dempster Dumpster sign, newspaper]

Poem 3:

[phrases cut from magazines]

Revising/Experimenting

Poem 1: I like the snake sign, but I'm going to change the line breaks.

**Note on Jake the Snake's Cage
on Tuesday at 9:00 a.m.**

Please don't tap or knock on
Jake's cage for the next 24 hours.
Jake gets jumpy after I feed him
a mouse.

Poem 2: I think I'll try a phrase from a cat food package instead of the dumpster sign. Poetry doesn't have to make complete sense. Sometimes it's okay to just play with words and elicit a chuckle.

Stormy

If some offensive
words escaped my
lips, let the storm-
winds blow them
hence. Just like cats'
teeth need special
care, the lamp of

fame casts a
fickle glow.

Poem 3: I don't like the collage poem, it's too hard to understand. I'll cut out more phrases and try again. I'll try a couple of them:

poetic sign language

EVERYBODY KNOWS:

if you don't

Stand up and shout.

GRAVITY SAYS YOU

Will Never Be
The Same.

Go fish

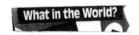

Which Way
Is Up?

Inside the Moon

IF YOU GO,
YOU'LL KNOW.

Stealaway

Please Hurry!

Final Drafts

See pages 93-96.

BIBLIOGRAPHY: FOUND POEM

ELEMENTARY SCHOOL

Lansky, Bruce. *Giggle Poetry, How to Write a Funny Found Poem*. Retrieved October 12, 2004 from **http://www.gigglepoetry.com/poetryclass/funnyfound.htm.**

MIDDLE SCHOOL AND HIGH SCHOOL

Dillard, Annie. *Mornings Like This: Found Poems*. New York: HarperCollins, 1995.

Found Magazine. Retrieved October 12, 2004 from **http://www.foundmagazine.com/.**

Heard, Georgia. "The Paper Trail," *A Kick in the Head*, selected by Paul B. Janeczko. Cambridge: Candlewick Press, 2005, pp. 42-43.

"in the awful seconds," *Class 324, Poetry*, Found Poem menu. Retrieved October 8, 2004 from **http://www.cqsb.qc.ca/svs/434/tpoetry.htm.**

Rothbart, Davy. *Found: The Best Lost, Tossed, and Forgotten Items from Around the World*. New York: Fireside, 2004.

Williams, William Carlos. "This is Just to Say." Retrieved October 8, 2004 from **http://www.cs.rice.edu/~ssiyer/minstrels/poems/274.html.**

17 FREE VERSE
Recommended for Grades K-12

BACKGROUND

In the 1600s, poets in France took the first steps to break loose from the strict rules of the existing poetry forms. In America, in 1855, the famous poet Walt Whitman wrote a break-through book of poems called *Leaves of Grass*. This book, which was written in free verse, did not follow the rules of any standard poetry forms. Along with Walt Whitman, one of the most revered American poets of free verse is William Carlos Williams who wrote a well-known poem, "The Red Wheelbarrow," about a wheelbarrow "glazed with rain water." Most of the poems written for adults today are free verse.

CHARACTERISTICS OF FREE VERSE

- With free verse, there are no rules, but it is not a free-for-all. The poet has to think carefully about every word, every line break, every thought.
- Free verse is often personal.
- Writing free verse can be similar to writing a paragraph, splitting it into lines of poetry, and eliminating unnecessary words.
- The poet decides where the line breaks should be. Lines can be of any length.
- The poem can be of any length.
- The poem does not rhyme.
- Each free verse poem has a rhythm or music of its own that makes sense to the poet.
- The rhythm can change throughout the poem. The poet may use short sharp sounds to make you read one section quickly, and she or he may use long sounds, that roll off your tongue, to make you read another section slowly.
- The language in free verse often includes strong imagery and poetic language such as *metaphor,* a comparison of two dissimilar things; *simile,* a comparison of two dissimilar things, using the word *like* or *as; alliteration,* repetition of a beginning consonant sound; *assonance,* repetition of a vowel sound; *consonance,* repetition of a final consonant; and *onomatopoeia,* words that sound like what they mean. (See Glossary page 213.)

EVERYDAY PARALLELS

Diary or journal entries are often similar to free verse, as are dream journals. Love letters are often written in free verse, and they have the personal tone that free verse commonly employs.

WHAT THIS FORM OFFERS

- Free verse introduces students to a conventional poetry form.
- It develops vocabulary.
- It provides an opportunity to use poetic language in a natural way.
- It gives students a venue for writing about personal issues.
- It offers students a chance to read expressively.
- It provides rich material for students to read and interpret—in the form of their own poems or those of master poets.
- It gives students the chance to relate to a poem on a personal level.

FREE VERSE

Storm

I hide
under
the blanket
when it's stormy.
Too much
noise.
Too much
light.
Too many
special effects
for me
and my dog, Ralphy

Metamorphosis

Do you ever wonder
if the caterpillar
knows what will
happen when she
builds a cocoon?

Does the resting pupa
realize what changes
are taking place
in the dark?

When the butterfly emerges,
does she remember
that she was once
a caterpillar crawling
on the ground?

Or does she think she's
always been able to
flit around on
paper-thin wings?

FREE VERSE

Mud Football

Mud sucked at
our bare feet
on the park ground,
soggy
with rain.

    Grunts
  snorts
guffaws
mixed with
spitting raindrops
and wind
in my ears.

Clutching the ball, I raced
down field till everyone
    piled on,
squooshing my
cheek into the sludge.

Nose filled with mud,
I wished we'd *never*
  get called home for dinner.

FREE VERSE

Kindergarten

Wearing matching dresses
Karen and I
were late to kindergarten
couldn't pull the heavy school door open
even when we yanked together
scurried around to the back of the school
saw two snarling dogs
fighting on top of a wild-eyed boy
ran back to the front door
pulled it open with our skinny arms

never told anyone about the boy

Ian

First Ian's sister drank.
Then she used coke.
Then she was in rehab.
Then she slipped.
Then she was back in rehab.

Ian's sister was center stage.
Always.
Until she left home.

Then Ian turned
Into the parents' project.
He wouldn't drink or take coke or go to rehab or slip or go back to rehab
or talk back or ask questions or shout obscenities or disobey.
He would play soccer
and study
and go to college
near home.

Ian's voice,
if you could call it that
turned mute as a moth
quiet as a koala
silent as a giraffe
until he'd lost himself
almost completely.

Think-through: My thoughts while writing "Mud Football"

First Thoughts

This is free verse so I'm not going to think about rhyme.

I'm going to tell a story in this poem, although free verse doesn't have to tell a story.

The poem will have a rhythm of its own, once I get started. I'll read it out loud to make sure it flows.

I'd like to write about a memory, but it'll probably be a memory of something my kids once did.

They used to go to the park and have pick up games of all kinds. They played hide-and-seek at night, they played baseball games with 4 people, and they had battles with squirt guns.

But I remember the time one of them came home covered with mud, with mud in every crevice. I wouldn't allow him in the house until he'd hosed off. He had played football at the park in a rainstorm.

Getting Started

I want to give some sensory impressions of what it was like playing the game. I'm picturing it.

> bare feet in the muddy field
> the sounds they would make
> what it would feel like to land in the mud
> how the kids must have felt about the experience

First Draft

> The mud sucked
> at our bare feet
> as we trampled the park
> ground, muddy with rain.
>
> The football flew
> between us, till
> it turned into a makeshift
> game of football
>
> Grunts, snorts, guffaws
> joined the sound of the wind and the
> rain spattering against a
> tin roof.
>
> I clutched
> the ball and raced down field
> till everyone piled on

grinding my cheek
into the mud

Nose filled with mud,
I wished we'd never have to stop.

Revising/Experimenting

It's too wordy.

I'll start to cut.

I'll take out the second stanza because it doesn't say anything about the senses, and I think it's clear what's happening from the title and the first stanza.

Even the last line in the first stanza could be cut—"as the football flitted between us."

Actually, the first stanza is too long and too filled with adjectives. It doesn't give the feeling of the scene. I'm going to take out "trampled."

> Mud sucked at
> our bare feet
> on the park
> ground, soggy
> with rain.

I'll take out the sound of rain on the tin roof because the kids would never hear it, and that image took away from the nitty gritty of the game. I'll change it to "spitting raindrops and wind in my ears." I like the repeated *i* sound in "spitting," "wind," and "in."

> Grunts
>   snorts
> guffaws
> mixed with
> spitting raindrops
> and wind
> in my ears.

I'll change the line breaks throughout, making the lines run on from one to the next, to keep the action moving. This will keep the reader reading at a rapid clip, which makes sense because this is a continuous game of football with no resting. I like the *s* sounds of "squooshing" and "sludge."

> Clutching the ball, I raced
> down field, till everyone
> piled on
> squooshing my
> cheek into the sludge.

I like the ending because it's unexpected that the kid would thoroughly enjoy a noseful of mud.

I'll change the title from "Memories of Mud Football" to "Mud Football." I like the alliteration of the first title, but it took away from the immediacy of the poem because it was too long.

Final Draft

See page 104.

Notes on Poems

Storm: There is repetition in the poem: "too much" is repeated 3 times. The blanket is under the word "under" on purpose.

Metamorphosis: Unanswerable questions can be good topics for poems. The underlying structure of the poem is that each stanza asks a question.

Mud Football: See the Think-through on page 106.

Ian: This poem is from a book I'm writing. The voice is a little older. I used similes in the last stanza. The line breaks are arranged for dramatic effect. The beginning is short and choppy. The longer lines reflect the backlash from Ian's parents.

Kindergarten: The kindergarten poem is about a memory. It's a little darker, which is typical of free verse, so I thought I'd include it.

BIBLIOGRAPHY: FREE VERSE

ELEMENTARY SCHOOL

Adoff, Arnold. *OUTside INside Poems.* New York: Lothrop, Lee and Shepard, 1981.

Adoff, Arnold. "Street Music," *Love That Dog* by Sharon Creech. New York: Joanna Cotler Books/HarperCollins, 2001.

Alarcón, Francisco X. *Laughing Tomatoes.* San Francisco: Children's Book Press, 1997.

Creech, Sharon. *Love That Dog.* New York: Joanna Cotler Books/HarperCollins, 2001.

Dotlich, Rebecca Kai. "A Place Called Prairie," *Home to Me, Poems Across America,* selected by Lee Bennett Hopkins. New York: Orchard Books, 2002, pp. 12-13.

Frost, Robert. "The Pasture," *Love That Dog* by Sharon Creech. New York: Joanna Cotler Books/HarperCollins, 2001.

Frost, Robert. "The Pasture." *Representative Poetry Online.* Retrieved October 26, 2004 from **http://eir.library.utoronto.ca/rpo/display/poem852.html.**

George, Kristine O'Connell. "At Night," *Old Elm Speaks.* New York: Clarion, 1998, p. 48.

George, Kristine O'Connell. "Bud," *Old Elm Speaks.* New York: Clarion, 1998, p. 7.

Giovanni, Nikki. *Spin a Soft Black Song.* New York: Farrar, Straus and Giroux, 1987.

Greenfield, Eloise. *Honey, I Love.* New York: Thomas Y. Crowell, 1978.

Hopkins, Lee Bennett. "No Matter," "Autumn's Beginning," "Winter," *Good Rhymes, Good Times!* New York: HarperCollins, 1995, pp. 18, 19, 27.

Kulling, Monica. "The Artist, Georgia O'Keefe" "Brave New Heights," *More Spice Than Sugar*, selected by Lillian Morrison. Boston: Houghton Mifflin, 2001, pp. 15, 50.

Moore, Lilian. "Scarecrow Complains," *The 20th Century Children's Poetry Treasury*, selected by Jack Prelutsky. New York: Alfred A. Knopf, 1999, p. 60.

Nye, Naomi Shihab, edited by. *Salting the Ocean: 100 Poems by Young Poets.* New York: Greenwillow, 2000.

Singer, Marilyn. "Burrows," "Dining Out," "Go-Betweens," "Natural Disasters," "Caves," "Back to Nature," "Patience," "Early Explorers," *Footprints on the Roof: Poems About the Earth.* New York: Alfred A. Knopf, 2002, pp. 6-7, 8, 10, 14-15, 18, 22, 38, 40.

Singer, Marilyn. "Dress-Up," "Lost and Found," "Rain Forest," "Wells," "The Moon's Gravity," *How to Cross a Pond: Poems About Water.* New York: Alfred A. Knopf, 2003, pp. 8, 12, 20, 32, 34.

Singer, Marilyn. "Fire-Bringers," "Forged," "Fire Fighters," "Birthday Party," "Distance from the Sun," *Central Heating: Poems About Fire and Warmth.* New York: Alfred A. Knopf, 2005, pp. 6, 12, 14, 22, 26.

Swados, Elizabeth. "Tough Kids," *Hey You! C'mere.* Arthur A. Levine Books, 2002, p. 8.

Weaver, Katie McAllaster. "Lullabies," *A Pet for Me*, selected by Lee Bennett Hopkins. New York: HarperCollins, 2003, p. 44.

Weaver, Katie McAllaster. "Oh, No!" *Oh, No! Where Are My Pants? and Other Disasters: Poems.* selected by Lee Bennett Hopkins. New York: HarperCollins, 2005.

Williams, William Carlos. "The Red Wheelbarrow," *Love That Dog* by Sharon Creech. New York: Joanna Cotler Books/HarperCollins, 2001.

Wilson, Sarah. *Beware the Dragons.* New York: Harper & Row, 1985.

Worth, Valerie. "Dog," *Love That Dog* by Sharon Creech. New York: Joanna Cotler Books/HarperCollins, 2001.

Worth, Valerie. "Lunchbox," *Pocket Poems*, selected by Bobbi Katz. New York: Dutton, 2004, p. 12.

Worth, Valerie. "Turtle," *All the small poems and fourteen more.* New York: Farrar, Straus and Giroux, 1994, p. 92.

ALL LEVELS

Creech, Sharon. *Heartbeat.* Joanna Cotler Books/HarperCollins, 2004.

Greenfield, Eloise. "Aunt Roberta," *Class 324*, Poetry, Lyrical Voice menu. Retrieved September 28, 2004 from **http://www.cqsb.qc.ca/svs/434/tpoetry.htm.**

Greenfield, Eloise. "The Seller," *Night on Neighborhood Street.* Dial Books for Young Readers, 1991.

Hesse, Karen. *The Cats in Krasinski Square.* New York: Scholastic, 2004.

Hughes, Ted. "The Harvest Moon," *The Earth Is Painted Green*, edited by Barbara Brenner. New York: Scholastic 1994, p. 57.

Myers, Walter Dean. "Love That Boy," *Love That Dog* by Sharon Creech. New York: Joanna Cotler Books/HarperCollins, 2001.

Myers, Walter Dean. *Harlem.* New York: Scholastic Press, 1997.

Roethke, Theodore. "The Waking," *The Earth Is Painted Green*, edited by Barbara Brenner.

New York: Scholastic, 1994, p. 42.

Wong, Janet S. *A Suitcase of Seaweed and Other Poems*. New York: Margaret K. McElderry Books, 1996.

Wong, Janet S. *The Rainbow Hand: Poems about Mothers and Children*. New York: Margaret K. McElderry Books, 1999.

MIDDLE SCHOOL AND HIGH SCHOOL

A-dae, Vena. "Pouring Milk Before Cereal." *Night Is Gone, Day Is Still Coming, stories and poems by American Indian teenagers and young adults,* edited by Betsy Franco. Cambridge: Candlewick Press, 2003, p. 33.

Baca, Jimmy Santiago. *Black Mesa Poems*. New York: New Directions, 1989.

Bly, Robert. "Driving to Town Late to Mail a Letter," *Poetry 180,* compiled by Billy Collins. Retrieved October 1, 2004 from **http://www.loc.gov/poetry/180/040.html**.

Childress, Jessie. "New Honesty," *Things I Have to Tell You, poems and writing by teenage girls,* edited by Betsy Franco. Cambridge: Candlewick Press, 2001, pp. 12-13.

Clifton, Lucille. "The Mississippi River Empties into the Gulf," *Modern American Poetry, Lucille Clifton: Online Poetry.* Retrieved October 1, 2004 from **http://www.english.uiuc.edu/maps/poets/a_f/clifton/onlinepoems.htm.**

Collins, Billy, *Poetry 180,* compiled by Billy Collins. Retrieved October 1, 2004 from **http://www.loc.gov/poetry/180.**

Collins, Billy, edited by. *Poetry 180.* New York: Random House, 2003.

Collins, Billy. "Advice to Writers," "Insomnia," "The Man in the Moon," "On Turning Ten," "Where I Live," *Sailing Alone Around the Room.* New York: Random House, 2002, pp. 8, 10, 34, 63, 130-131.

Collins, Billy. "Introduction to Poetry," *Poetry Daily.* Retrieved September 28, 2004 from **http://www.poems.com/intro_lo.htm.**

Collins, Billy. *Link Library, Poems by Billy Collins.* Retrieved October 4, 2004 from **http://www.bigsnap.com/linklibrary.html#poembypoem.**

Collins, Billy. "On Turning Ten," *Billy Collins, Poems.* Retrieved October 4, 2004 from **http://www.bigsnap.com/p-ad-02.html.**

de la Mare, Walter. "The Snowflake," *The 20th Century Children's Poetry Treasury,* selected by Jack Prelutsky. New York: Alfred A. Knopf, 1999, p. 10.

Foster, Mahogany Elaj. "I'm Sayin'," "Words," *Things I Have to Tell You, poems and writing by teenage girls,* edited by Betsy Franco. Cambridge: Candlewick Press, 2001, pp. 6, 56.

Giovanni, Nikki. *Grand Fathers*. New York: Henry Holt, 1999.

Giovanni, Nikki. "Knoxville, Tennessee," *My America,* selected by Lee Bennett Hopkins. New York: Simon & Schuster, 2000, p. 23.

Giovanni, Nikki. *Quilting the Black-Eyed Peas.* New York: William Morrow, 2002.

Glenn, Mel. *Foreign Exchange*. New York: Morrow Junior Books, 1999.

Glenn, Mel. *The Taking of Room 114.* New York: Lodestar Books, Dutton, 1997.

Glenn, Mel. *Who Killed Mr. Chippendale?* New York: Lodestar Books, Dutton, 1996.

Glenn, Mel. *Split Image.* New York: HarperCollins 2000.

Grover, Lorie Ann. *On Pointe.* New York: Margaret K. McElderry Books, 2004.

Hall, Quantedius. "Time Somebody Told Me," from *You Hear Me? poems and writing by teenage boys,* edited by Betsy Franco. Cambridge: Candlewick Press, 2000, p. 1.

Henry, Erin B. "My Heart Is in My Throat," *Things I Have to Tell You, poems and writing by teenage girls,* edited by Betsy Franco. Cambridge: Candlewick Press, 2001, p. 5.

Hesse, Karen. *Out of the Dust.* New York: Scholastic, 1997.

Hesse, Karen. *Witness.* New York, Scholastic, 2001.

Koch, Kenneth. "Mountain." *Poemhunter.com, Kenneth Koch.* Retrieved October 4, 2004 from **http://www.poemhunter.com/p/m/poem.asp?poet=12369&poem=343967.**

Koertge, Ron. *Shakespeare Bats Cleanup.* Cambridge: Candlewick Press, 2003.

Laidlaw, Brian. *Quarter-Life, Poems and Music, 2004.* **www.brianlaidlaw.com.**

Mendoza, Marcel. "Just because I love darkness . . . ," from *You Hear Me? poems and writing by teenage boys,* Cambridge: Candlewick Press, 2000, p. 4.

Rhode Island Department of Administration, Library Services. *Titles for YART Discussion: Recent Poetry for Teens.* Retrieved August 12, 2005 from **http://www.lori.ri.gov/youthserv/yart/ya_poetr.php.**

Rosaldo, Renato. *Prayer to Spider Woman/Rezo a la mujer araña.* Saltillo, Coahuila, Mexico: Instituto Coahuilense de Cultura, 2003.

Sones, Sonya. *What My Mother Doesn't Know.* New York: Simon Pulse, 2003.

Soto, Gary. *A Fire in My Hands.* New York: Scholastic, 1990.

Soto, Gary. *Canto Familiar.* New York: Harcourt, 1995.

Stone, Miriam. *At the End of Words, a daughter's memoir.* Cambridge: Candlewick Press, 2003.

Stone, Miriam. "To Live," *Things I Have to Tell You, poems and writing by teenage girls,* edited by Betsy Franco. Cambridge: Candlewick Press, 2001, p. 58.

Whitman, Walt. "Leaves of Grass," *Leaves of Grass.* Retrieved October 18, 2004 from **http://www.whitmanarchive.org/archive1/works/leaves/1856/text/ww/ frameset.html.**

Williams, William Carlos. "The Red Wheelbarrow." Retrieved October 4, 2004 from **http://www.writing.upenn.edu/~afilreis/88/wcw-red-wheel.html.**

Wong, Janet S. *Behind the Wheel: Driving Poems.* New York: Margaret K. McElderry Books, 1999.

Yeahpau, Thomas M. "The Gap," *Night Is Gone, Day Is Still Coming, stories and poems by American Indian teenagers and young adults,* edited by Betsy Franco. Cambridge: Candlewick Press, 2003, p. 24.

18 HAIKU, SENRYU, RENGA
Recommended for Grades K-12

BACKGROUND

Hundreds of years ago in Japan, poets held parties during which they wrote a form of poetry called *renga.* Someone would be asked to write a short first stanza called *hokku,* and other poets would take turns writing the next verses, linking each verse to the previous one in subtle ways. Writing a renga could take all night. At one point in history, some of the starting verses, the *hokku,* were published and called *haiku.* Some famous masters of *haiku* are Bashō, Buson, and Issa. *Senryu* (SEN-dree-yoo; the *dree-yoo* is said very quickly) which also originated with *renga* is similar to *haiku,* but it is humorous and the subject matter is often human nature.

CHARACTERISTICS OF HAIKU

- Haiku is about small, ordinary, everyday things.
- It's like a snapshot or observation of a moment in time. The moment is usually in the present.
- The subject of the haiku is traditionally something in nature, and the poem hints of a season.
- Haiku does not rhyme.
- It is commonly written in incomplete sentences.
- Punctuation and capitalization are optional.
- The language is simple and straightforward, often without adjectives, metaphors, or similes.
- Haiku often has three lines—the first and third lines are short and the second line is longer.
- People often think that haiku must have three lines with the following syllables in each line: 5, 7, 5, or a total of 17 syllables. This formula is optional. Haiku written in Japanese is usually the same length as 12 to 15 English syllables, so 17 syllables is actually a little long.

CHARACTERISTICS OF RENGA AND SENRYU

- Renga has a 3-line stanza followed by a 2-line stanza. This repeats over and over, commonly 12 times, but as many as 1,000.
- Often the 3-line stanza has a similar line length to a haiku (5, 7, 5 syllables), and the 2-line stanza has 7 syllables in each line. (7, 7)
- It is usually written by multiple poets, with poets taking turns writing stanzas.
- One poet starts with 3 lines and sets the scene.

- Each poet relates his or her stanza to the previous one by echoing the subject, an image, a sound, or a word (or play on a word) in the previous stanza. The poet can also echo the previous stanza by relating to the opposite of the subject, any image, or word of the stanza.
- The subject matter and season can change from stanza to stanza; the links are subtle.
- The ending stanza is often uplifting or hopeful and sometimes includes an *-ing* form of the verb.
- Senryu has a similar structure to haiku, but it is often about human nature and is usually humorous.
- The stanzas of a renga can be about nature like haiku and/or can be humorous like senryu.

FOR OLDER POETS

Try writing a renga after writing haiku. Students can write in groups of 3 or 4.

EVERYDAY PARALLELS

When rappers have a rap-off, it's similar to a linked renga since they take turns reacting to each other. When hiking or on a walk, people often have haiku-like experiences, noticing something about a flower, an insect, the raindrops in a puddle—as if taking a mental picture of a moment. Photographers often capture an image that is like a visual haiku. Cartoons sometimes have captions that sound a bit like senryu. Also, *honko* written on subjects such as cats or dogs, office etiquette, or e-mail is a popular spin-off from senryu.

WHAT THESE FORMS OFFER

- Haiku, senryu, and renga introduce conventional poetry forms.
- They offer a chance to appreciate small things.
- They are short and highly accessible to all students.
- They teach economy of words, which is useful when writing any form of poetry.
- These forms help students learn how to look for, observe, remember, and imagine vivid details—an important skill in all poetry writing.
- They give insight into another culture.
- Writing in groups for the renga can be very stimulating and opens poets' minds to new ways of writing and new subjects to write about.

HAIKU

lines of small black ants
come back for the cookie crumbs
next to my bare feet

crickets harmonize
with a chorus of tree frogs—
free summer concert

HAIKU

Mysteriously
the silkworm moths are forming.
Metamorphosis!

White dandelion
full of lacy parachutes—
I make the same wish.

SENRYU

E-mail piling up
So hard to find the jewels
Camouflaged by spam!

RENGA

the wren takes a dip
in a puddle of spring water
fluffing her feathers

In the mirror, my moussed-
up hair enjoys its new look

muddy reflection
in the moss choked pond water
swallows flying above

I'll shave the sides of my hair
the sun can polish my head

missed morning sunrise
too busy writing haiku
about other things

My haiku assignment fell
in the swimming pool. Ker-pliff!

water striders skim
across the water's surface
making small circles

My tomcat Scarface chases
red leaves in drifting spirals

a scar on my arm
left over from last year's sting
by a tiny bee

Being in the here and now
Stinging snowflakes on my tongue

apples are rotting
a leaf falls past my window
last night, an orange moon

Sundogs wag their tails at me;
My heart is a sun, leaping.

Betsy Franco and Maria Damon

Think-through: My thoughts while writing the renga with Maria Damon

First Thoughts

I'll just write a renga by myself, pretending I'm two different people.

Hmm, now that I've done this by myself, I can see that it would be more exciting to write with someone else, with at least one other person.

I'll ask my friend, poet Maria Damon, to write it with me.

I'll send her my chapter on haiku and renga so she knows what I'm going for.

I'll write a 3-line haiku (syllables: 5, 7, 5) and she can write a 2-line stanza (syllables: 7, 7) that relates to it in some way. Then we'll keep repeating this pattern until we feel that we're done.

Getting Started

I'll read rengas in several books. Here's one where Bashō, the most famous haiku master, wrote with two other poets in Japan hundreds of years ago.

I can see by reading this that the stanzas can relate to each other in very subtle ways, that the seasons can change throughout the renga, that the subject matter can be similar to haiku (nature) or senryu (human nature).

I'll start with this stanza:

> the wren takes a dip
> in a puddle on the lawn
> fluffing her feathers

Revising/Experimenting

I'm going to revise the first stanza so the season is more obvious before I send it to Maria:

> the wren takes a dip
> in a puddle of spring rain
> fluffing her feathers

Writing Linked Stanzas

While writing my stanzas of the renga (every other one) it helps if I get in touch with what's going on around me, such as the sun coming up, the cat cleaning herself, or the sound of the garbage truck. This helps me stay in the present and keep my images simple.

I also get ideas from the stanzas that Maria writes. A word or image or idea or the sound of words in her stanza will jog a memory or a thought.

When linking with Maria's stanza the first link that comes to me is always a link to a specific word. Sometimes I let that idea go and link to a sound or an idea. Or I purposely link to an image, idea, or sound that is the opposite of hers, to keep things interesting.

I also try to write both haiku and senryu, about nature and human nature, to change the tone of the stanzas.

I consciously don't write in sentences, just phrases, and I don't use many adjectives or adverbs.

Specific Links

1. I started with a reference to spring and an image of a bird fluffing her feathers.

2. Maria linked to the word "fluffing" in my first stanza, but she wrote a senryu about looking in the mirror at "moussed-up hair." She also linked "puddle" to "mirror" since both reflect.

3. I made a link to the word "mirror" by talking about a muddy reflection in a pond.

4. Maria played with the s sound of "swallows" by using the words "shave," "sides," and "sun." She also linked "polish" to my word "reflection."

5. I transformed the word "sun" into "sunrise" and talked about being too busy writing haiku, I missed the sunrise.

6. Maria picked up on the word "haiku" and changed the subject to haiku homework falling in the swimming pool.

7. I saw an image of water in her reference to a swimming pool and wrote about water striders.

8. Maria picked up on the word "circle" in my stanza and kept up the geometric reference by using "spirals" in her stanza.

9. Maria talked about a cat named Scarface, so I changed it to a scar on my arm, from a bee sting.

10. Maria talked about "stinging" snowflakes on her tongue to relate to my words "bee sting."

11. Maria's stanza referred to the "here and now" so I decided to make the link an opposite. My stanza talks about a leaf falling "past" my window. I used the word "past" in opposition to the "here and now" but I used a different sense of the word "past."

12. Maria ended by opposing my "moon" with a "sun." When light in the atmosphere plays on dust, drops of water, or ice crystals, it creates the optical image of a halo. This is called a "sundog." She played on that word in a fanciful way, saying that the sundogs were wagging their tails. Maria ended with an uplifting image and the -ing form of a verb, which is traditional.

Conclusions

It was much more fun to write with someone because the poem went in directions I could never have expected. It was more like a game or an adventure.

Notes on Poems

Haiku: I tried to put a subtle hint of a season in each: bare feet mean summer, dandelions are spring, and silkworms are spring.

Senryu: I thought e-mail was a down-to-earth topic, more appropriate for a senryu. Getting outraged by spam lends some humor to it.

Renga: See Think-through on page 118.

Final Draft

See page 117.

BIBLIOGRAPHY: HAIKU, SENRYU, RENGA

ELEMENTARY SCHOOL

Chisoku. "The face of the dragonfly . . . ," *Eric Carle's Animals Animals.* New York: Philomel Books, 1989, p. 82.

Demaru. "Butterflies dancing through falling snow! . . . ," *Eric Carle's Animals Animals.* New York: Philomel Books, 1989, p. 12.

Franco, Betsy. "Haiku," *Counting Our Way to the 100th Day!* New York: Margaret K. McElderry Books, 2004, p. 39.

Gaki. "Haiku," *Tomie dePaola's Book of Poems,* edited by Tomie dePaola. New York: G.P. Putnam's Sons, 1988, p. 19.

George, Kristine O'Connell. "Poaching," "Broken String," *Old Elm Speaks.* New York: Clarion, 1998, pp. 31, 47.

Greenfield, Eloise. "Neighborhood Street,", "The House with the Wooden Windows," *Night on Neighborhood Street.* New York: Dial Books for Young Readers, 1991.

Issa. "How sadly the bird in his cage . . . ," *Eric Carle's Animals Animals.* New York: Philomel Books, 1989, p. 13.

Koson. "Leaping flying fish! . . . ," *Eric Carle's Animals Animals.* New York: Philomel Books, 1989, p. 11.

Kyorai. "Galloping pony . . . ," *Eric Carle's Animals Animals.* New York: Philomel Books, 1989, p. 75.

Prelutsky, Jack. *If Not for the Cat.* New York: Greenwillow, 2004.

Schenk de Regniers, Beatrice, et. al. *Sing a Song of Popcorn.* New York: Scholastic, 1988, pp. 127-132.

Singer, Marilyn. "11 a.m. in Japan," *Nine O'Clock Lullaby.* New York: HarperCollins, 1991.

Singer, Marilyn. "Spring in the Garden," *How to Cross a Pond: Poems About Water.* New York: Alfred A. Knopf, 2003, p. 14.

Yaku. "A discovery! . . . ," *Eric Carle's Animals Animals.* New York: Philomel Books, 1989, p. 82.

Yayû. "Haiku," *Tomie dePaola's Book of Poems,* edited by Tomie dePaola. New York: G.P. Putnam's Sons, 1988, p. 78.

ALL LEVELS

Buson. "Spring Rain," *A Kick in the Head,* selected by Paul B. Janeczko. Cambridge: Candlewich Press, 2005, p. 14.

George, Kristine O'Connell. "First day, . . . ," *A Kick in the Head,* selected by Paul B. Janeczko. Cambridge: Candlewick Press, 2005, p. 16.

Gollub, Matthew. *Cool Melons Turn to Frogs: The Life and Poems of Issa.* New York: Lee & Low Books, 1998.

Yolen, Jane and Jason Stemple. *Least Things: Poems About Small Natures.* Honesdale, Pennsylvania: Boyds Mills Press, 2003.

MIDDLE SCHOOL AND HIGH SCHOOL

Hass, Robert, edited by. *The Essential Haiku.* Hopewell, New Jersey: The Ecco Press, 1994.

Janeczko, Paul B. and J. Patrick Lewis. *Wing Nuts, Screwy Haiku.* New York: Little, Brown and Company, 2006.

Janeczko, Paul B., selected by. *Stone Bench in an Empty Park.* New York: Orchard Books, 2000.

Koertge, Ron. "Just a single space . . . ," "I know we broke up . . . ," *Shakespeare Bats Cleanup.* Cambridge: Candlewick Press, 2003, pp. 7, 47. ["I know we broke up . . ." is senryu]

Lewis, J. Patrick. "The spider . . . ," "The meadow," "Skeleton elms . . . ," *Black Swan, White Crow.* New York: Atheneum, 1995.

Stone, Miriam. "Your Presence," "For a Walk with My Grandmother," *At the End of Words, a daughter's memoir.* Cambridge: Candlewick Press, 2003, pp. 32-33, 36.

Van Den Heuvel, Cor. edited by. *The Haiku Anthology.* New York: Simon and Schuster, 1986.

19 LIMERICK
Recommended for Grades K-12

BACKGROUND

No one knows for sure where the limerick originated. Some think it was first used in *Mother Goose Melodies* published in 1719. Others think it originated in France and was brought to the town of Limerick, Ireland by Irish soldiers returning home from war. Regardless, it has lasted through the centuries. Edward Lear made it popular in 1846 with his collection, *A Book of Nonsense*. Since his time, the last line of the limerick has become more surprising than it used to be. The ending usually includes some sort of twist.

CHARACTERISTICS OF A LIMERICK

- The limerick is a light form of poetry.
- It is often nonsensical and humorous.
- It consists of 5 lines.
- The rhyme scheme is AABBA. (The first, second, and fifth lines rhyme. The third and fourth lines rhyme.)
- The rhythm is something people usually pick up by reading a number of limericks out loud.
  There are three beats in lines 1, 2, and 5, and two beats in lines 3 and 4.
  da da DA, da da DA, da DA
  da da DA, da da DA, da DA
  da da DA, da da DA
  da da DA, da da DA
  da da DA, da da DA, da DA
  The formal name for "da da DA" is *anapestic* and the formal name for "da DA" is *iambic*. (See *meter* in Glossary.)
- The poem often starts with a phrase such as:
  There was an old lady from Spain. . .
  A handsome young man from New York. . .
  A boy with a puppy named Joe. . .

EVERYDAY PARALLELS

Nursery rhymes, jump rope rhymes, and autograph album verse have the flavor of the limerick. They are all light verse.

WHAT THIS FORM OFFERS

- The limerick introduces a conventional poetry form.

- It is a light, fun form of poetry.
- The rhythm is familiar to most students.
- It offers an opportunity to play with rhyme in a light-hearted way. Even nonsense rhymes can be effective in this form.
- It is a good form for musical learners because of its strong beat.
- It encourages students to think of a twist or surprise at the end, which is an element of most poetry.

LIMERICK

There was a red rooster named Paul
who was sick of his morning call.
He changed "doodle doo"
to a quack and a moo and
his new call woke no one at all!

There's a family in Aberdeen.
They have so many kids they could scream.
No one gets much attention.
But, wait, did I mention,
they formed their own basketball team!

A farm boy once came from the south,
who wanted cold milk from his cows.
He fed them some ice
which worked out quite nice.
He's working on chocolate milk now.

LIMERICK

Miss Jennifer Brown was renowned.
Not a spot in her house could be found.
She kept her place clean
with obsessive routines,
even vacuumed her old Basset hound.

I knew a young lady named Tyne.
Early curfews to her were a crime.
She set the clocks back
so her parents lost track.
But she's never at classes on time.

Think-through: My thoughts while writing the limerick about a big family

First Thoughts

I'll look through my folder of interesting poetry ideas I've collected.

There are lots of ideas about cats and dogs in here but I've done enough animal poems.

Here's an idea: several friends came from big families and I've always wanted to write something about that.

Getting Started

I'll write about a family that has lots of kids. First I'll say the drawbacks and then I'll say the fun part, which is that they could play lots of sports without gathering anyone else.

First Draft

> There once was a family named Stall.
> There were 22 fine kids in all.
> They fought for attention.
> There was no "alone time."
> They formed one soccer team in the fall.

> or

> They made two soccer teams in the fall.

> or

> They could play real soccer each day.

Revising/Experimenting

This obviously needs work because the rhythm is off and I didn't rhyme lines 3 and 4.

First I'll make it funnier by saying "They had so many kids they could scream."

Now I have to rhyme with "scream." But that rhymes with "team!"

Now I have to rhyme the first line with "scream" and "team:"
> "I know a big family in Aberdeen."

But the rhythm is off.

How about "There's a family in Aberdeen."

For lines 3 and 4, the word "mention" rhymes with "attention."

> "No one gets much attention
> But, wait, did I mention,"

For the last line, here are some possibilities:
> They formed their own basketball team!

By themselves, they had two soccer teams!

By themselves, they formed two soccer teams!

The second one is more to the point. They could play without anyone else showing up.

The third one is hard to say when I say it aloud.

But the first one has the best rhythm, and limericks are slightly nonsensical anyway.

Final Draft

See page 125.

BIBLIOGRAPHY: LIMERICK

ELEMENTARY SCHOOL

Anonymous. "There Was a Young Lady of Niger," "A Mouse in Her Room," *Talking Like the Rain,* selected by X.J. Kennedy and Dorothy M. Kennedy. New York: Little, Brown and Company, 1992, p. 41.

Espy, Willard R. "My TV Came Down with a Chill," *Talking Like the Rain,* selected by X.J. Kennedy and Dorothy M. Kennedy. New York: Little, Brown and Company, 1992, p. 43.

Franco, Betsy. "Hats," *Counting Our Way to the 100th Day!* New York: Margaret K. McElderry Books, 2004, p. 16.

Katz, Bobbi. "Hector McVector," "Lydia Luce," *A Rumpus of Rhyme.* New York: Dutton, 2001.

Kennedy, X.J. *Uncle Switch: Loony Limericks.* New York: Margaret K. McElderry Books, 1997.

Lear, Edward. "There Was an Old Man with a Beard," *Talking Like the Rain,* selected by X.J. Kennedy and Dorothy M. Kennedy. New York: Little, Brown and Company, 1992, p. 40.

Lewis, J. Patrick. "The End of the Bookworm's Feast," *The Bookworm's Feast.* New York: Dial Books, 1999.

Singer, Marilyn. "Count Dracula," *Monster Museum.* New York: Hyperion, 2001, p. 70.

Singer, Marilyn. "There Once Was a Golden Retriever," *It's Hard to Read a Map with a Beagle on Your Lap.* New York: Henry Holt, 1993.

ALL LEVELS

Livingston, Myra Cohn, selected by. *Lots of Limericks.* New York: Margaret K. McElderry Books, 1991.

Scotellaro, Robert. *Dancing with Frankenstein and Other Limericks.* East Riding of Yorkshire, England: Hand's Up Books, 2003. See **www.handsup.karoo.net,** retrieved January 24, 2005, or e-mail: handsup@handsup.karoo.co.uk.

MIDDLE SCHOOL AND HIGH SCHOOL

Asimov, Isaac and John Ciardi. *Limericks.* New York: Gramercy, 2000.

Cerf, Bennett, compiled by. *Bennett Cerf's Out on a Limerick.* New York: HarperCollins, 1987.

Herrick, Steven. "There once was limerick called Steven...," *A Kick in the Head,* selected by Paul B. Janeczko. Cambridge: Candlewick Press, 2005, p. 21.

Lear, Edward. *The Complete Verse and Other Nonsense* edited by Vivien Noakes. New York: Penguin, 2001.

Lear, Edward. "There was an Old Lady whose folly...," *A Kick in the Head.* Cambridge: Candlewick Press, 2005, p. 20.

20 LIST POEM
Recommended for Grades K-12

BACKGROUND

The list poem or catalog poem consists of a list or inventory of things. Poets started writing list poems thousands of years ago. They appear in lists of family lineage in the *Bible* and in the lists of heroes in the Trojan War in Homer's *Iliad*. About 250 years ago, Christopher Smart wrote a famous list poem about what his cat Jeoffrey did each morning. It starts with the cat inspecting his front paws and ends with the cat going in search of breakfast. "Cat Bath" on page 132 is a very simple version of the poem about Jeoffrey. The famous American poet Walt Whitman is known for the extensive lists in his poetry.

CHARACTERISTICS OF A LIST POEM

- A list poem can be a list or inventory of items, people, places, or ideas.
- It often involves repetition.
- It can include rhyme or not.
- The list poem is usually not a random list. It is well thought out.
- The last entry in the list is usually a strong, funny, or important item or event.

EVERYDAY PARALLELS

Throughout history, people have kept an inventory of things, from ancestors to possessions. Most everyone is familiar with a grocery list, a homework list, a holiday wish list, and a list of chores. David Letterman is famous for his lists of 10 items on topical subjects. Some popular songs are lists—of positive attributes of a lover, of trials and tribulations, of ways to lose a lover, and more.

WHAT THIS FORM OFFERS

- The list poem introduces a conventional poetry form.
- It is a very accessible form that is easy and natural for students of all ages to write.
- It lends itself to students' interests or passions, so they can use it to tell their stories.
- It presents a repetitive, sometimes patterned format, in some poems more extensively than others.
- It offers an opportunity to think and talk about sequencing, in the context of a list that is meaningful to a student.

LIST POEM

Cat Bath

She licks her neck.
She licks her nose.
She licks her legs.
She licks her toes.
She licks her tummy,
She licks her back.

Then she rubs my leg
to ask for a snack.

On the Way to School

I find a dark brown penny.
I pat a friendly cat.
I slosh through murky puddles.
I stomp a berry flat.

I tap tap tap with a pointy stick
on a fence along the block.
I move a roly poly bug
and kick a bright white rock.

And when I hear the first bell ring
I know I might be late.
I sprint like a racer, full-speed ahead
and whizz through the school gate!

LIST POEM

Signs of Fall

When summer is departing
and fall is arriving,
the wind whips through the trees
and spooks the cat.
The leaves consider
wearing bold new colors.
In the corner of my room
my mother builds a pile
of new notebooks and pencils and paper.
And when I bike past the school,
I start hoping my new teacher
isn't too strict
and that my friends and I
are all assigned to the same class.

LIST POEM

Home

Home is where you
can shrug off your
backpack and your

worries, sling around
your complaints about
impossible questions on the science
test, and supposedly
best

friends, fling your smelly
clothes and your towel on
the floor after a stinging hot

shower, splay on the
couch and flick off
your mind with the

remote, brag
like a hyena about
the goal that just
nipped the

goal post, and just be
yourself (but eventually, you have to explain your test grade, lose the
argument that TV enhances your homework skills, and especially
pick up "those filthy clothes and that wet towel that's ruining the
carpet. This minute—you heard me!" I do, anyway.)

Think-through: My thoughts while writing "Home"

First Thoughts

In my idea files, I had a list of ideas of things that parents nag their kids about:

      loud music
      homework
      curfew
      too much time playing video games
      being late in the morning to get to school

Some of these topics will appear in other poems, I'm sure.

Getting Started

I think I'll write about the dichotomy between what you wished home was like and what it was really like when you were a teenager.

You wanted to relax. In some ways you could and in some ways you couldn't. I'll write about what I nagged my sons about.

First Draft

Home Is Where

Home is the place
where you drop
your backpack
and your stories
and your dirty clothes
and your troubles
and your used towels
and just be yourself

(but mom always makes you put away
the backpack, clothes, and towels.
At least my mom does.)

Revisions/Experimentation

I like this poem and I might use it for a younger collection, but this is way too young and not complex enough poetry-wise for middle/high school so I'll change the verbs and play with the line breaks.

I'll make the lines break so that the stanzas run into each other—so that a thought from one stanza is completed in the next stanza. That will force the reader to read on. I'll also end every line in the poem at a place that makes the reader go to the next line.

Home Is Where

Home is where you
can shrug off your
backpack and your

worries, sling around
your complaints about
impossible questions on the math test, big
brothers, and supposedly
best

friends, fling your dirty
clothes and your towel on
the floor after a stinging hot
shower, splay on the
couch and flick off
your mind with the

remote control, dismiss
the glare that Jimmy zapped
your way when
you blamed him in front of

Pam, brag like a hyena about
the goal that just
nipped the

goal post, and just be
yourself (but inevitably you have to explain why the math test was
so impossible, flick off the TV until all homework is in the can. And
especially pick up those dirty clothes and that wet towel.)

I'm going to take out the references to the older brother and to Jimmy, the friend, because I'm starting to see a story line where the kid is coming home following an after-school soccer game and the other references are superfluous.

I need to work on the ending to make it feel like an ending. I want it to be more funny than depressing. I'll change "inevitably" to "eventually." I'll put it in quotes so it sounds like the mom is telling the kid to pick things up in a nagging tone. I'll add, "At least I do." to lighten the mood and make it feel like an ending.

New last stanza:

> . . . and just be
> yourself (but eventually you have to explain why the math test was
> so impossible, flick off the TV until all homework is done, and especially, pick up "those dirty clothes and that wet towel that's ruining
> the wood floor. Right now!" At least I do.)

136

The ending seems too young, so I'll heighten the attitude a little.

> . . . and just be
> yourself (but eventually, you have to explain your test grade, lose
> the argument that TV enhances your homework skills, and especial-
> ly pick up "those filthy clothes and that wet towel that's ruining the
> carpet. This minute—you heard me!" I do, anyway.)

Final Draft

See page 134.

Notes about Poems

Cat Bath: This is a classic list poem because there is repetition. I hope students
don't think they have to rhyme. It would be better if they didn't. I wrote at least
a dozen drafts to get this right.

On the Way to School: I tried to bring in lots of senses: textures (of a cat), sounds
(*slosh, stomp, tap, ring, whizz*). The sounds are all onomatopoetic, or words that
mean what they sound like.

Signs of Fall: I purposely didn't rhyme this poem. I tried to build strong images
that are signs of fall. I changed the verbs to "whips," "spooks" and "builds" to
make them more intriguing.

Home: See the Think-through on page 135.

BIBLIOGRAPHY: LIST POEM

ELEMENTARY SCHOOL

Anonymous. "Old Noah's Ark," *Tomie dePaola's Book of Poems*, edited by Tomie dePaola.
New York: G.P. Putnam's Sons, 1988, p. 61.

Brown, Margaret Wise. *Good Night, Moon*. New York: HarperCollins, 1947.

Brown, Mikel D. "Berry Paints," *Night Is Gone, Day Is Still Coming, stories and poems
by American Indian teenagers and young adults*, edited by Betsy Franco. Cambridge:
Candlewick Press, 2003, p. 21.

Dotlich, Rebecca Kai. "Let's Talk," *Wonderful Words*, selected by Lee Bennett Hopkins.
New York: Simon & Schuster, 2004, p. 22.

Dotlich, Rebecca Kai. "Marvelous Math" *Marvelous Math*, selected by Lee Bennett Hopkins. New York: Simon & Schuster, 1997, p. 6.

Dotlich, Rebecca Kai. "What Is Science?" *Spectacular Science*, selected by Lee Bennett
Hopkins. New York: Simon & Schuster, 1999, p. 10.

Farjeon, Eleanor. "Cats," *The 20th Century Children's Poetry Treasury*, selected by Jack
Prelutsky. New York: Alfred A. Knopf, 1999, p. 51.

Florian, Douglas. "The Bullfrog," *lizards, frogs, and polliwogs*. New York: Harcourt, 2001,
p. 42.

Franco, Betsy. "One Hundred Sparklers," *Counting Our Way to the 100th Day!* New York: Margaret K. McElderry Books, 2004, p. 22.

Giovanni, Nikki. "mommies," "daddies," "two friends," "shirley and her son," "springtime," *Spin a Soft Black Song.* New York: Farrar, Straus and Giroux, 1987, pp. 11, 13, 25, 29, 39.

Greenfield, Eloise. "Riding on the Train," "By Myself," *Honey, I Love.* New York: Thomas Y. Crowell, 1978.

Hopkins, Lee Bennett. "Behind the Museum Door," "Good Books, Good Times!" *Good Rhymes, Good Times!* New York: HarperCollins, 1995, pp. 6, 28.

Katz, Bobbi. "Spring Conversations," "Summer Jazz," "Parade," "Sea Speak," *A Rumpus of Rhyme.* New York: Dutton, 2001.

Lewis, J. Patrick. "Home Poem (or, The Sad Dog Song)," *Pocket Poems,* selected by Bobbi Katz. New York: Dutton, 2004, p. 23.

McKleod, Kris Aro. "How to Paint a Summer Day," *Whatever the Weather,* written and edited by Betsy Franco. New York: Scholastic, 2001, p. 24.

McNaughton, Colin. "Transylvania Dreaming," *Making Friends with Frankenstein.* Cambridge: Candlewick Press, 1994, p. 78.

Merriam, Eve. "Places to Hide a Secret Message," *Tomie dePaola's Book of Poems,* edited by Tomie dePaola. New York: G.P. Putnam's Sons, 1988, p. 49.

Prelutsky, Jack. "Twaddletalk Tuck," "I'm Sorry!" "There's a Worm in My Apple," "I Am Sitting Here and Fishing," *Something Big Has Been Here.* New York: Greenwillow, 1990, pp. 64, 93, 106-107, 112-113.

Shapiro, Arnold L. "I Speak, I Say, I Talk," *Tomie dePaola's Book of Poems,* edited by Tomie dePaola. New York: G.P. Putnam's Sons, 1988, p. 64.

Silverstein, Shel. "Magic," "Flag," "Listen to the Mustn'ts," I'm Making a List," "Hector the Collector," "Sick," "Recipe for a Hippopotamus Sandwich," "Eighteen Flavors," *Where the Sidewalk Ends.* Harper & Row, 1974, pp. 11, 24, 27, 37, 46-47, 58-59, 115, 116.

Singer, Marilyn. "Ears," "Fur," "Tails," *It's Hard to Read a Map with a Beagle on Your Lap.* New York: Henry Holt, 1993, pp. 4-5, 16-17, 30-31.

Singer, Marilyn. "Underwater Ballet," "Ocean Checklist," *How to Cross a Pond: Poems About Water.* New York: Alfred A. Knopf, 2003, p. 22.

Soto, Gary. "Eating While Reading," selected by Jack Prelutsky. New York: Alfred A. Knopf, 1999, p. 87.

Swados, Elizabeth. "Summer," "Aunt Evelyn," *Hey You! C'mere.* Arthur A. Levine Books, 2002, pp. 13, 18-19.

Viorst, Judith. "Mother Doesn't Want a Dog," *Eric Carle's Animals Animals.* New York: Philomel Books, 1989, p. 60.

Viorst, Judith. "Some Things Don't Make Any Sense at All," *Tomie dePaola's Book of Poems,* edited by Tomie dePaola. New York: G.P. Putnam's Sons, 1988, p. 53.

Worth, Valerie. "Dog," *Love That Dog.* New York: Joanna Cotler Books/HarperCollins, 2001.

Worth, Valerie. "sweets," "pocket," *All the Small Poems and Fourteen More.* New York: Farrar, Straus and Giroux, 1994, pp. 125, 193.

Yolen, Jane. "Shepherd's Night Count," *Talking Like the Rain,* selected by X.J. Kennedy and Dorothy M. Kennedy. New York: Little, Brown and Company, 1992, p. 87.

ALL LEVELS

Harley, Avis. "Slug File," *A Kick in the Head,* selected by Paul B. Janeczko. Cambridge: Candlewick Press, 2005, p. 51.

MIDDLE SCHOOL AND HIGH SCHOOL

Agam, Idit Meltzer. "As a child I was taught . . . ," *Things I Have to Tell You, poems and writing by teenage girls,* edited by Betsy Franco. Cambridge: Candlewick Press, 2001, p. 2.

Billy, Ramona. "I Am Native American," *Night Is Gone, Day Is Still Coming, stories and poems by American Indian teenagers and young adults,* edited by Betsy Franco. Cambridge: Candlewick Press, 2003, p. 85.

Gillam, Julia. "It's not the size that counts," *Things I Have to Tell You, poems and writing by teenage girls,* edited by Betsy Franco. Cambridge: Candlewick Press, 2001, p. 38.

Glenn, Mel. "Annamarie Parisi," *Who Killed Mr. Chippendale?* New York: Lodestar Books, 1996, p. 92.

Glenn, Mel. "Clyde Dunston," *Split Image.* New York: HarperCollins, 2000, p. 64.

Glenn, Mel. "Derek Bain," "Morton Potter," *The Taking of Room 114.* New York: Lodestar Books, Dutton, 1997, pp. 54, 98.

Joans, Ted. "Watermelon," *The Earth Is Painted Green,* edited by Barbara Brenner. New York: Scholastic, 1994, p. 43.

Koch, Kenneth. "One Train May Hide Another," "The Boiling Water," "To Various Persons Talked to All At Once." Retrieved October 4, 2004 from **http://www.poemhunter.com/kenneth-koch/poet-12369/**.

Schonborg, Virginia. "Coney," *Celebrate America in Poetry and Art.* published in association with The National Museum of American Art, Smithsonian Institution. New York: Hyperion, 1994, p. 80.

Soto, Gary. "How to Sell Things," *A Fire in My Hands.* New York: Scholastic, 1990, pp. 21-22.

Yeahpau, Thomas M. "Oral Tradition," *Night Is Gone, Day Is Still Coming, stories and poems by American Indian teenagers and young adults,* edited by Betsy Franco. Cambridge: Candlewick Press, 2003, p. 87-89.

21 MULTI-VOICE POEM
Recommended for Grades K-12

BACKGROUND

As far back as the Greeks, plays have been written in verse, with many parts and a chorus. One of the famous Greek playwrights was Sophocles, who wrote the tragedy *Oedipus the King*. Through the ages, there have been many plays in verse, most notably the work of William Shakespeare. Operas have also been written in verse and often the singers are singing different words at the same time.

These plays and operas in verse could be said to be the forerunners of the multi-voice poem, or its subset, the dialogue poem. Paul Fleischman is a famous children's author who has written outstanding books of multi-voiced poems. His book, *Joyful Noise: Poems for Two Voices*, won the Newbery Award in 1989.

CHARACTERISTICS OF A MULTI-VOICE POEM

- The multi-voice poem has two or more voices.
- The poem is at its best when it is read aloud.
- The voices can be having a conversation.
- The voices can speak separately and/or at the same time.
- When they speak together, they don't have to be saying the same thing.
- The language can be informal and colloquial.
- The voices can be people, inanimate objects, places or abstract ideas. A pair of socks can talk to their owner, a cat can talk to a dog, a boy can talk to his feelings of jealousy, the sun can talk to the moon.
- The poem is formatted on the page so that it is obvious when each voice joins in. There are many ways to do this. For example, each voice can be written on a different side of the page. Or the poet can boldface the part of one of the voices if there are two voices, or color code the voices if there are more than two.

EVERYDAY PARALLELS

Sometimes Reader's Theater is written in verse to be recited in classrooms. A dinner conversation in which everyone is talking at once is similar to a multi-voice poem in which the speakers overlap. An ordinary, casual conversation between several people often has overlaps as well. In addition, when observing or listening to an orchestra or quartet in music, you can see and hear that the musicians, or groups of musicians, take turns and overlap in the way a multi-voice poem does. Rap, hip-hop, and pop music often have two voices.

WHAT THIS FORM OFFERS

- Multi-voice poetry introduces a semi-conventional poetry form.
- It enables students to practice writing dialogue.
- It encourages students to empathize with and get into the persona of whoever or whatever is talking.
- It encourages playfulness in writing.
- The subject matter can vary widely, according to students' interests.
- Writing multi-voice poetry can be a prequel to playwriting or screen-writing.
- It is excellent for "socially intelligent" students because it is about interacting, and it needs to be read aloud.
- It helps students with fluency.

MULTI-VOICE POEM

Hey, Tooth

Hey, tooth
time to come out.

Don't wiggle so hard.
Oooooo. Ouch.

Time to let go.
Did you hear what I said?

I'm hanging on
by a very thin thread.

There! You're out!
Yay! Yippeeee!

Now you can trade
with the Tooth Fairy!

MULTI-VOICE POEM

Spider Above the Bathtub

I'm just a little arachnid.

I guess you could call yourself that.

I'm comfortable in the bathroom.

Get out of my habitat!

This corner is perfect for my web
and a great place to lay my eggs.

I beseech you to leave, invading beast.
What? Do I have to beg?

I'm staying put, and remember,
you're the predator, not the prey.

If you won't leave, I'm out of here.
I guess I'll stay dirty today!

MULTI-VOICE POEM

Feet Get a Say

Hey, you,

        Look down!

Take notice
You don't seem

        to appreciate
our unique talents: our unique talents:
We
step one

        at a time
but we work   but we work
in tandem   in tandem
to take you   to take you
wherever

        you're going.
By the way,   By the way,
where are

        you going?
Never mind—   Never mind—
Too charged

        a subject.
Back

        to the point.
We're stuck   We're trapped
inside putrid   inside sweaty
shoes   socks
when   when
we'd much rather   we'd much rather
spend time

        barefoot
in grass.   in sand.
And why in the world?

        did you
have to

        go out for track?
We're
pooped   sore
we hurt   we ache
and we crave   and we crave
couch time.   couch time.
More importantly

        when will
you pass

        your damn driver's test
and give us   and give us
a break?   a break?

Think-through: My thoughts while writing "Spider above the Bathtub"

First Thoughts

I could write a conversation between two people, or a person and an animal, or a kid and her backpack.

There could be some conflict involved.

Maybe two siblings who share a room.

Maybe a kid trying to catch a frog and take it home.

My neighbor is afraid of spiders. I wonder what would happen if there was a spider in her bathtub. My kids always have me come and get the spiders out of the bathroom for them.

Getting Started

I'll write about two siblings, one is afraid of spiders and the other isn't. But the one who isn't afraid is not willing to help—just wants to give advice and watch her sibling squirm.

I'll picture the scene. The spider is up in the corner of the ceiling. She's made a web, she's laid her eggs in an egg sac and there are tiny black spots on the tub where she's dropped her food (Is that what those little black dots are? There's always a mess under the web.)

I'll rhyme the poem to begin with—for fun.

There are lots of potential rhyming words: *habitat* and *prey* are easy to rhyme with, *legs* and *eggs, spider* and *beside her* are potential rhymes. I don't think the rhyme will be forced.

But I hope kids writing their own poems won't rhyme.

First Draft

(The unhelpful sibling is in plain text. The other sibling afraid of spiders is in bold face.)

It's just a little spider.
Call it whatever you want.
It's set up house in the bathroom. Just capture it in a cup.
Get it out of my habitat!
Just cover it with a paper cup and a piece of cardboard.
But watch out for its legs.
I beseech you to get it out of here.
Do I have to beg?
I've gotta run but remember,
you're the predator, not the prey.
Well bye then. I am out of here.
I guess I'll stay dirty today.

Revising/Experimenting

Now I'm going to revise.

I like the tone of the poem, kind of sassy.

But when I read it over, I got confused about who was talking.

Maybe I'll have the spider speak instead of one of the siblings.

Also, I need to work on the rhyme and rhythm and make the words more exactly what I mean.

I'll change "spider" to "arachnid."

I'll say, "I beseech you to leave, invading beast" to heighten the drama. I won't have to deal with this paper cup/cardboard explanation of how to capture a spider if I make the spider talk. The spider could talk about how the bathtub is a great place for laying eggs. That makes it grosser.

Spider above the Bathtub

I'm just a little arachnid.

I guess you could call yourself that.

I'm comfortable in the bathroom.

Get out of my habitat!

This corner is perfect for my web
and a great place to lay my eggs.

I beseech you to leave, invading beast.
What? Do I have to beg?

I'm staying put, and remember
you're the predator, not the prey.

Well, if you won't leave, I'm out of here.
I guess I'll stay dirty today!

Final Draft

See page 144.

Notes on Poems

Hey, Tooth: This poem has a light tone. It's a conversation between a child and a tooth. I made it rhyme for fun, but I wouldn't suggest that for students' poems.

Feet Get a Say: I tried to make this interesting to read. Some of the phrases are said by one voice, some by two, and sometimes the voices say different things at the same time.

Spider Above the Bathtub: See Think-through on page 146.

BIBLIOGRAPHY: MULTI-VOICE POEM

ELEMENTARY SCHOOL

Anonymous. "Five Little Chickens," *Side by Side, Poems to Read Together* collected by Lee Bennett Hopkins. New York: Simon & Schuster, 1988, p. 37.

Anonymous. "The Three Little Kittens," *Side by Side, Poems to Read Together* collected by Lee Bennett Hopkins. New York: Simon & Schuster, 1988, p. 18.

Coatsworth, Elizabeth. "Roosters," *Eric Carle's Animals Animals*. New York: Philomel Books, 1989, p. 84.

Dotlich, Rebecca Kai. "You and Me," *Climb into My Lap*, selected by Lee Bennett Hopkins. New York: Simon & Schuster, 1998, p. 34.

Franco, Betsy. "How We Made 100," *Counting Our Way to the 100th Day!* New York: Margaret K. McElderry Books, 2004, p. 38.

Greenfield, Eloise. "Goodnight, Juma," *Night on Neighborhood Street*. New York: Dial Books for Young Readers, 1991.

Harrison, David L. *Farmer's Garden: Poems for Two Voices*. Honesdale, Pennsylvania: Boyds Mills Press, 2000.

Hoberman, Mary Ann. *You Read to Me, I'll Read to You*. New York: Little, Brown and Company, 2001.

Martin, Jr., Bill. *Brown Bear, Brown Bear, What Do You See?* New York: Henry Holt, 1983.

McNaughton, Colin. "It Was a Day Like Any Other in Fishtown," *Making Friends with Frankenstein*. Cambridge: Candlewick Press, 1994, p. 47.

Merriam, Eve. "Five Little Monsters," *Side by Side, Poems to Read Together* collected by Lee Bennett Hopkins. New York: Simon & Schuster, 1988, p. 36.

Prelutsky, Jack. "Hello! How are you? I am fine!," *Something Big Has Been Here*. New York: Greenwillow, 1990, p. 36.

Singer, Marilyn. "Dr. Jekyll and Mr. Hyde," *Monster Museum*. New York: Hyperion, 2001, pp. 16-17.

Swados, Elizabeth. "Me," *Hey You! C'mere*. Arthur A. Levine Books, 2002, p. 37-41.

MIDDLE SCHOOL AND HIGH SCHOOL

Fleischman, Paul. *Big Talk: Poems for Four Voices*. Cambridge: Candlewick, 2000.

Fleischman, Paul. *I Am Phoenix: Poems for Two Voices*. New York: HarperCollins, 1989.

Fleischman, Paul. *Joyful Noise: Poems for Two Voices*. New York: HarperCollins, 1992.

Glenn, Mel. "Lana and Yana," "Jessica, Lisa," *Split Image*. New York: HarperCollins, 2000, pp. 19, 132.

Glenn, Mel. "Lynette and Patti," "Derek and Rhonda," "Harry Balinger and Frank Bicardi," *The Taking of Room 114*. New York: Lodestar Books, Dutton, 1997, pp. 1, 2, 28.

Koertge, Ron. "Poetry, Poetry, Everywhere," "Weather Report: E-Mail Flurries, with Slight Accumulation," "Venice (California)," "Hotmail," "The Surprise," "Almost

Home," *Shakespeare Bats Cleanup*. Cambridge: Candlewick Press, 2003, pp. 80, 81, 85, 91-92, 93-94, 111-112.

Lewis, J. Patrick. "Double Doubles," *Vherses: Poems for Outstanding Women*. Mankato, Minnesota: Creative Editions, 2005.

Yolen, Jane and Heidi E.Y. Stemple. *Dear Mother, Dear Daughter*. Honesdale, Pennsylvania: Boyds Mills Press, 2001.

22 ODE
Recommended for Grades K-12

BACKGROUND

An ode is a poem in praise of something. In Greek, ode means "to sing." Thousands of years ago, a Greek poet named Pindar is said to have invented the ode. He wrote odes in very noble language, to Greek athletes and other subjects. Pindar's odes were meant to be read in public by a chorus. The Roman poet Horace also wrote odes, but they were more personal and reflective. Originally, odes were written in praise of important people, events, or things, and followed strict rules about stanzas and rhythm. But in modern odes, poets sometimes write about ordinary people or objects, and they do not adhere to strict rules. Some notable odes by Pablo Neruda are written to his socks and to watermelons.

CHARACTERISTICS OF AN ODE

- The ode is a poem in praise of something.
- It describes what is or was wonderful about a person, a thing, a place, an event, or an abstract idea such as friendship or "hanging out."
- Many odes include some exaggeration.
- The poet often speaks directly to the object or person, such as "Oh, baseball cap."
- The poem is often written in a way that shows it is very deeply felt and that the subject matter has been carefully considered.
- It can include rhyme or not.
- It can be any length.

EVERYDAY PARALLELS

Children and adults sometimes speak glowingly about something they love—a pet, a new mitt, a new scooter, a TV show, a car, or a book. An advertisement can be similar to an ode. When a speaker is introduced in an assembly, his or her accomplishments and strong points are summarized in a way that is similar to the ode.

WHAT THIS FORM OFFERS

- The ode introduces a conventional poetry form.
- It requires students to contemplate an object or person in depth.
- It gives students a reason to include rich details and description.
- It encourages students to organize their thoughts and be persuasive.

- It offers a context for students to tell what they value and why.
- The form invites the use of comparisons (simile, metaphor).
- Any subject can be used, from admirable people to cell phones.
- The ode offers an opportunity to personify an object, by speaking to it.
- It gives students a chance to interweave reasoning and emotion.
- The loose restrictions make the ode easy to write.
- It offers a wide range of possibilities as far as the tone of the poem, from silly to straightforward to serious.

ODE

Ode to Grandma

Soft cheek,
warm hands.
Listens, listens
to me.
Makes me
toast with
peanut butter,
and cuts
the bread
into
thin deliciously
sloppy strips.

ODE

Ode to My Baseball Cap

Baseball cap, you're a perfect shade of red,
perched like a bird on the crown of my head.

Your beak shades my face from harmful rays
and keeps it dry on rainy days.

You block out the sun when a fly ball's hit
so I catch the ball with a *thud* in my mitt.

And most important, you deserve a prize,
when you hide my bad haircuts from staring eyes!

ODE

Ode to My Cell Phone
written outside chemistry class

Without you
I'm
nobody—
drifting alone,
un-
anchored.

More than aluminum
  computer chips
    sound waves
      (or whatever you're made of),
you and your sappy tune
reassure me that
  somebody knows
    I'm somewhere.

You knock down barriers
so I can talk to
friends
no matter where,
as if we had
tin cans
  con-
    nected
      by
    a
  string.

Unless
I forget to give you
juice,
you never desert me.

Wait. Hold on a minute.
I'll keep singing
your praises
as soon as I take this . . .

"Hullo."

Think-through: My thoughts while writing "Ode to My Baseball Cap"

First Thoughts

An ode is supposed to praise something, so I need to think of a topic. The poet Pablo Neruda wrote an ode to his socks. Maybe a piece of clothing would be a good topic, but I'll stay open.

It would be helpful to visit the school around the corner from my house where I can observe the children and see what they value:

> I see a boy hugging a dog good-bye.
> I see a girl carefully folding up her scooter.
> I see a girl with a backpack with multiple trinkets hanging off of it.
> I see a boy with a well-worn baseball cap.

Let me think back to what I cherished as a child and what my children were attached to—a hat, a jean jacket, special socks, a favorite T-shirt, a dog, a cat, their "junk boxes," action figures.

Getting Started

I'm going to choose a piece of clothing after all—a baseball cap! It was hard to get my own boys to take off their baseball caps, and when I was a teacher, children wanted to keep their caps on (especially after a haircut), even though it was against the rules.

I'm going to picture the details in my mind. I'll think about when, where, how, why, who? I'll scribble down details I remember.

> My notes: color, logo, rainy days, haircuts, baseball games

Time to ask myself some questions: What's so great about a cap? What's so great about its appearance? What does it do for a kid? Why do kids get attached to their caps? How are caps useful for a kid?

I'm going to start writing about four basic ideas, in four different stanzas. I'll put the most surprising idea at the end.

First Draft

> Oh, my cap,
> your cardboard beak
> protects me from the sun
> and keeps my face dry during rain showers.
>
> > or
>
> Your sturdy beak
> protects me
> My cap
> the perfect colors,
> the blue of the ocean,
> the white of a spring cloud

When a fly ball comes my way,
you shield me from the sun
so I can make an out
and you keep my face dry
during a rain shower.

And most important, my cap,
you are like a friend
and hide a bad haircut
from staring eyes.

Revising/Experimenting

Now I'm going to experiment.

I'm definitely going to talk to the cap as if it were alive. I'm going to try rhyme, but I won't keep the rhyme if it sounds forced.

It's time to work on the words and images.
- I'd better delete words that were just okay and make them more specific. (I'll put "shades my face from harmful rays" instead of "protects me from the sun.")
- Can I add one of the senses? I'll add a sound ("with a *thud* in my mitt").
- What does the hat look like when I picture it in my mind's eye? I'll add a simile ("perched like a bird on the crown of my head").
- Time to tighten up the words. (A cap is not really "like a friend," protecting me "from staring eyes." Friends don't often do that. I'll take that out.)

I'll divide the lines so it's in couplets, in which every two lines rhyme.
I ended up writing about five drafts of this poem.

Final Draft

See page 154.

Notes on Poems

Ode to Grandma: I wrote many of the lines so that you need to go on to the next line to finish the thought. I did this to emphasize the child's enthusiasm for Grandma.

Ode to My Baseball Cap: See Think-through on page 156.

Ode to My Cell Phone: I tried to have a slightly sassy, yet lonely tone. I thought carefully when I chose the words "sappy" and "unanchored." I tried to make the layout of the poem reflect the meaning. For example, the word "unanchored"is split in two. The part about a tin-can phone is written in a way that looks like a string between two phones.

BIBLIOGRAPHY: ODE

ELEMENTARY SCHOOL

Adoff, Arnold. "Chocolate Chocolate," *The 20th Century Children's Poetry Treasury*, selected by Jack Prelutsky. New York: Alfred A. Knopf, 1999, p. 74.

Aiken, Joan. "Rhyme for Night," *Talking Like the Rain*, selected by X.J. Kennedy and Dorothy M. Kennedy. New York: Little, Brown and Company, 1992, p. 84.

Alarcón, Francisco X. "My Grandma's Song," "Ode to Corn," "A Tree for César Chávez," *Laughing Tomatoes*. San Francisco: Children's Book Press, 1997, pp. 9, 15, 24.

Anonymous. "Queen Nefertiti," *Talking Like the Rain*, selected by X.J. Kennedy and Dorothy M. Kennedy. New York: Little, Brown and Company , 1992, p. 70.

Conkling, Hilda. "Dandelion," *Tomie dePaola's Book of Poems*, edited by Tomie dePaola. New York: G.P. Putnam's Sons, 1988, p. 71.

Giovanni, Nikki. "yvonne," "poem for debbie," "mattie lou at twelve," "springtime," *Spin a Soft Black Song*. New York: Farrar, Straus and Giroux, 1987, pp. 28, 33, 39, 53.

Greenfield, Eloise. "Harriet Tubman," *Honey, I Love*. New York: Thomas Y. Crowell, 1978.

Kirk, Daniel. "Master, I Love You!," *Dogs Rule*. New York: Hyperion, 2003, p. 18.

Nash, Ogden. "The Octopus," *Eric Carle's Animals Animals*. New York: Philomel Books, 1989, p. 14.

Sundgaard, Arnold. "The Elephant," *Eric Carle's Animals Animals*. New York: Philomel Books, 1989, p. 31.

Wong, Janet S. "Noodles," *The 20th Century Children's Poetry Treasury*, selected by Jack Prelutsky. New York: Alfred A. Knopf, 1999, p. 74.

Worth, Valerie. "back yard," *Tomie dePaola's Book of Poems*, edited by Tomie dePaola. New York: G.P. Putnam's Sons, 1988, p. 33.

Worth, Valerie. "raw carrots," *All the small poems and fourteen more*. New York: Farrar, Straus and Giroux, 1994, p. 22.

ALL LEVELS

Soto, Gary. "Ode to Pablo's Tennis Shoes," *A Kick in the Head*, selected by Paul B. Janeczko. Cambridge: Candlewick Press, 2005, pp. 34-35.

MIDDLE SCHOOL AND HIGH SCHOOL

Bates, Katherine Lee. from "America the Beautiful," *Celebrate America in Poetry and Art*. published in association with The National Museum of American Art, Smithsonian Institution. New York: Hyperion, 1994, p. 10.

Clifton, Lucille. "Praise Song." *Poetry 180*, compiled by Billy Collins. Retrieved October 12, 2004 from **http://www.loc.gov/poetry/180/015.html**.

Glenn, Mel. "Father Francis Bosco, Angela Falcone, Guidance Counselor," "Harry Balinger, Detective, Angela Falcone, Guidance Counselor," *Who Killed Mr. Chippendale?* New York: Lodestar Books, 1996, pp. 15, 30-31.

Hughes, Langston. "Helen Keller," *The Collected Poems of Langston Hughes*. New York: Vintage Books, 1994, pp. 146.

Johnson, Stephan. "First Love," "Floating, for Adrien," "Song for My Father," *You Hear Me? poems and writing by teenage boys*, edited by Betsy Franco. Cambridge: Candlewick Press, 2000, pp. 70, 92-93, 95.

Landin, Rigo. "Ode to My Hair Tail," *You Hear Me? poems and writing by teenage boys*, edited by Betsy Franco. Cambridge: Candlewick Press, 2000, p. 18-19.

Lion Shows, Destiny Starr. "Little Grandma," *Night Is Gone, Day Is Still Coming, stories and poems by American Indian teenagers and young adults*, edited by Betsy Franco Cambridge: Candlewick Press, 2003, p. 62.

Neruda, Pablo. *Full Woman, Fleshly Apple, Hot Moon*. New York:HarperFlamingo, 1998.

Soto, Gary. *Neighborhood Odes*. New York: Harcourt Brace Jovanovich, 1992.

Soto, Gary. "That Girl," *A Fire in My Hands*. New York: Scholastic, 1990, pp. 15-16.

Stone, Miriam. "For Dad," *At the End of Words, a daughter's memoir*. Cambridge: Candlewick Press, 2003, pp. 44-45.

Taylor, Shuysuanne. "Words on Hands," *You Hear Me? poems and writing by teenage boys*, edited by Betsy Franco. Cambridge: Candlewick Press, 2000, p. 49-50.

23 PERSONA POEM
Recommended for Grades K-12

BACKGROUND

At least as far back as the ancient Greeks, poets have talked about whose voice is speaking in the poem. Is it the poet's true voice or has the poet created a character to speak through? If the poem is in first person, does it really reflect the poet's true feelings?

In a form or mode of poetry called the persona poem or "mask poem," the poet takes on the voice of someone else—puts on a mask. In these poems, the poet takes over the persona of someone other than himself or herself and speaks in the first person. In the 1800s Robert Browning and Alfred Lord Tennyson wrote persona poems, among other forms. These poets and their contemporaries usually took on the voice of a historical or mythological character. This is also done in modern persona poems, but nowadays, poets also speak as if they were such things as an object, a place, an animal, an abstract idea, or a fantasy character.

CHARACTERISTICS OF A PERSONA POEM

- The poet often takes on the persona of an object, animal, place, or abstract idea.
- The speaker can also put on the mask of another person, such as a fantasy or historical person, or anyone other than himself. This could include someone the poet knows, such as his father.
- The poem is written in the first person.
- If non-human, the entity speaks as if it's human.
- The poem can be serious and/or humorous.
- It can include rhyme or not.
- It can be any length.

EVERYDAY PARALLELS

When students "feel for" other students, or have empathy for them, they are getting into someone else's skin. Playing a role in a play, playing charades, doing impersonations, or mimicking someone is akin to writing a persona poem. Sometimes people make off-hand comments that hint at taking on another persona: "I wish I were my cat. Then I would sleep all day." "I'd hate to be my soccer socks and live next to my stinky feet."

WHAT THIS FORM OFFERS

- The persona poem introduces a conventional poetry form.
- It encourages students to write from a different point of view.
- It can encourage compassion.
- The poem allows students to get into "someone else's skin," to see things from another perspective.
- It encourages use of specific detail.
- It works well with a wide range of tones, from humorous to somber.

PERSONA POEM

Plea from a Jacket

You take me off
and toss me around
Whenever it's hot
I land on the ground.

I know you love me
but every spring
I end up in the Lost and Found!

PERSONA POEM

The Peach

I did it—formed a flower this year.
I'll be a summer peach for sure.

The whoosh of wind—I'm clinging tight.
The raindrops pelt me through the night.

The calico kitty leaps near me
but doesn't catch the chickadee.

I thought that cat would knock me down,
that scruffy, predatory clown.

I'm yellow-white, like midnight's moon.
Don't pick me yet, it's still too soon.

Warmed by the sun, I'm nearly ripe,
wrapped in a coat of fuzzy white.

If you don't grab me quickly, girl
you'll lose me to some scrappy squirrel.

PERSONA POEM

Darkness, My Darkness

I paint
blackness
all around you—

I brush
up against you,
reminding you
I'm a hiding
place for
bats,
apparitions, and
other shadow-
lovers,

I set a special place
for silence
at my table,

but open my arms
to music and
generously
carry
the sound.

I offer a roster
ranging
from kicking back
to full-out rowdiness,

and keep my promise that
anything
can happen.

Think-through: My thoughts while writing "The Peach"

First Thoughts

I could write a poem from the perspective of a backpack, a flag, or something else found at school.

Or I could take on the persona of a pet or a wild animal or a threatened animal.

I'm looking out the window at that almost-ripe peach I'm hoping the squirrels won't eat before it's ready to pick. Maybe I'll write a poem as if I'm the peach.

Getting Started

I'm going to brainstorm some things the peach might be thinking: It could worry about rain, squirrels, my cat Jada jumping for birds right near it, a peach near it crowding it out, not being watered, rain threatening to knock it off.

I could start when it first forms a flower that turns into the peach.

I haven't written in couplets very much (only in "Ode to My Baseball Cap" on page 154 and the first riddle about water on page 173) so I'll write in couplets and rhyme every 2 lines in this poem.

First Draft

The Peach

I did it—formed a flower this time.
was determined to produce a peach sublime.

Through rain and wind, I clung on tight,
or when hefty birds would dare alight.

The kitty stalked, then pounced near me
to catch the little chickadee.

I thought she'd knock me off my perch.
made me tremble, shake, lurch.

I'm yellow, small, not time to pick
I'd taste too _____ and tart

but now I'm pink, all fuzzy white
I'm ready now, just about ripe.

If you don't pick me quickly, girl,
I'll be the meal for a squirrel.

Revising/Experimenting

I'll write it in the present as the peach goes through different stages, instead of in the past tense.

I don't like the beginning stanzas. They seem a little stilted and forced. Need to make them smoother, even if the rhyme is more predictable.

> I did it!—formed a flower this year.
> I'll be a summer peach for sure.
>
> The whoosh of wind—I'm clinging tight.
> The rain is pelting through the night.

I need to work on the rhythm, sharpen the images, make the language more natural.

> This morning, kitty leaped near me
> but didn't catch the chickadee.
>
> I thought that cat would knock me down,
> that scruffy, predatory clown.

[Lots of hard *c* sounds together in "cat," "knock," and "clown." That's good.]

> I'm yellow-white, like a midnight moon
> Don't pick me yet, it's still too soon.
>
> or
>
> My taste is tart, it's still too soon.
>
> Warmed by the sun, I'm nearly ripe,
> wrapped in a coat of fuzzy white.
>
> or
>
> Warmed by sunlight, nearly ripe,
> I'm wrapped in a coat of fuzzy white.

[Lots of *w* sounds in "warmed," "wrapped," "white"]

For the last stanza, I'll jazz it up a bit.

> If you don't pick me quickly, girl
> you'll lose me to some scrappy squirrel.

["Pick" and "quickly" have *ck*; "scrappy squirrel" is fun to say.]

Final Draft

See page 164.

Notes on Poems

Plea from a Jacket: The surprise in the poem is the last line about ending up in the Lost and Found.

The Peach: See Think-through on page 166.

Darkness, My Darkness: I wanted to do a persona poem about something more nebulous, more abstract. So instead of writing a persona poem about nighttime, I called it "Darkness, My Darkness." That way, it could be about nighttime as well as the internal shadow-side of a person. The mood is supposed to be intriguing, mysterious. I tried to create this mood with words like "apparitions," "silence," "anything can happen." I used lots of *s* sounds in the stanza about music.

BIBLIOGRAPHY: PERSONA POEM

ELEMENTARY SCHOOL

Alarcón, Francisco X. "Prayer of the Fallen Tree," *Laughing Tomatoes*. San Francisco: Children's Book Press, 1997, p. 30.

Florian, Douglas. "The Skink," "The Tortoise," "The Komodo Dragon," "The Gila Monster," "The Box Turtle," "The Glass Frog," "The Wood Frog," "The Spring Peepers," *lizards, frogs, and polliwogs*. New York: Harcourt, 2001, p. 6, 8, 18, 20, 22, 34, 38, 46.

George, Kristine O'Connell. "Oaks Introduction," "Old Elm Speaks," *Old Elm Speaks*. New York: Clarion, 1998, pp. 4, 48.

Giovanni, Nikki. "fear," "poem for ntombe iayo (at five weeks of age)," *Spin a Soft Black Song*. New York: Farrar, Straus and Giroux, 1987, p. 5.

Hesse, Karen. *The Cats in Krasinski Square*. New York: Scholastic Press, 2004.

Hughes, Langston. "Mother to Son," *Tomie dePaola's Book of Poems*, edited by Tomie dePaola. New York: G.P. Putnam's Sons, 1988, p. 55.

Janeczko, Paul B., selected by. *Dirty Laundry Pile*. New York: HarperCollins, 2001.

Katz, Bobbi. "Paper Dreams," *A Kick in the Head*, selected by Paul B. Janeczko. Cambridge: Candlewick Press, 2005, pp. 44-45.

Katz, Bobbi. "Bumptious Burps," "Washing Machine," "The Wind," "We're Crows," *A Rumpus of Rhyme*. New York: Dutton, 2001.

Kirk, Daniel. *Dogs Rule*. New York: Hyperion, 2003.

Lear, Edward. "The Pelican Chorus," *Eric Carle's Animals Animals*. New York: Philomel Books, 1989, pp. 68-69.

McNaughton, Colin. "Billy Boy McCoy," "Ogre My Dead Body! (The Ogre's Song)," *Making Friends with Frankenstein*. Cambridge: Candlewick Press, 1994, pp. 14, 34.

Sierra, Judy. *Antarctic Antics*. New York: Gulliver Books, Harcourt Brace & Company, 1998.

Singer, Marilyn. *All We Needed to Say*. New York: Atheneum, 1996.

Singer, Marilyn. *Fireflies at Midnight*. New York: Atheneum, 2003.

Singer, Marilyn. "Frankenstein's Monster," *Monster Museum.* New York: Hyperion, 2001, p. 14.

Singer, Marilyn. *The Company of Crows.* New York: Clarion Books, 2002

Singer, Marilyn. "The Fly," *Creature Carnival.* New York: Hyperion, 2004, p. 26.

Singer, Marilyn. *Turtle in July.* New York: Macmillan, 1989.

ALL LEVELS

Creech, Sharon. *Heartbeat.* Joanna Cotler Books/HarperCollins, 2004.

Dickinson, Emily. "Bee! I'm expecting you!" *Poemhunter.com: Emily Dickinson.* Retrieved October 4, 2004 from **http://www.poemhunter.com/p/m/poem.asp?poet=3053&poem=46922.**

MIDDLE SCHOOL AND HIGH SCHOOL

Damron, Angela. "When We Are Gone," *Night Is Gone, Day Is Still Coming, stories and poems by American Indian teenagers and young adults,* edited by Betsy Franco. Cambridge: Candlewick Press, 2003, p. 120.

Glenn, Mel. *Foreign Exchange.* New York: Morrow Junior Books, 1999.

Glenn, Mel. *The Taking of Room 114.* New York: Lodestar Books, Dutton, 1997.

Glenn, Mel. *Who Killed Mr. Chippendale?* New York: Lodestar Books, Dutton, 1996.

Glenn, Mel. *Split Image.* New York: HarperCollins, 2000.

Grimes, Nikki. *Bronx Masquerade.* New York: Dial Books, 2002.

Hesse, Karen. *Out of the Dust.* Scholastic, 1997.

Hesse, Karen. *Witness.* New York, Scholastic, 2001.

Jarrell, Randall, "The Death of the Ball Turret Gunner." Retrieved August 19, 2005 from **http://www.poemhunter.com/P/M/poem.asp?poet=9054&poem=174480.**

Katz, Bobbi. *We the People.* New York: Greenwillow, 2000.

Koertge, Ron. *Shakespeare Bats Cleanup.* Cambridge: Candlewick Press, 2003.

marquis, don. *archy and mehitabel.* Garden City, New York: Anchor Books, 1973.

24 RIDDLE
Recommended for Grades K-12

BACKGROUND

The riddle, an ancient poetry form, goes all the way back to sanskrit. Riddles are universal. They are written throughout the world and in many diverse cultures. Some riddles, called folk riddles, consist of a simple question and answer. They are usually light and whimsical. Others, called literary riddles, are usually longer poems. Some of these are as formal as sonnets and have abstract answers such as death or knowledge.

CHARACTERISTICS OF A RIDDLE

- The riddle usually involves a question and an answer.
- The question is misleading, and the answer is surprising.
- The question often involves:
  a pun or play on words ("black and white and red all over/read all over"—newspaper),
  a metaphor ("when all of nature changes to formal gowns but has nowhere to go but down"—fall)
  conflicting metaphors ("as solid as bone, as fluid as blood, as vaporous as breath"—water)
  a contradiction/paradox ("It's a shell all over but you won't find it beach combing"—an egg)
- The riddle can involve an object that is personified (speaking like a person) and is describing itself: "I am as fast as . . ."
- In its simplest form, it can consist of two or three hints and a question. It can also be a long, sophisticated poem.
- It can include rhyme or not.
- It can be any length.

EVERYDAY PARALLELS

In everyday conversation, people ask each other, "Guess what happened to me at . . .?" Children's games, such as "20 questions," "I Spy," and "Charades" involve guessing. Popsicle sticks and bubble gum wrappers sometimes have riddles printed on them. In kindergarten classes, children may be asked to bring in a mystery item beginning with the letter of the week so that the class can guess its identity from hints the child gives. Greeting cards are often riddles. Mystery novels are lengthy riddles, and detectives and forensic scientists look for clues to solve "crime riddles."

WHAT THIS FORM OFFERS

- The riddle introduces a conventional poetry form.
- It allows for personification, in which an object speaks.
- Writing and solving riddles provides opportunities for logical reasoning and critical thinking.
- The riddle introduces older students to the idea of paradox/contradiction, metaphor, and punning.
- Creating and answering riddles is fun.

FOR OLDER STUDENTS

Encourage longer poems involving metaphor or paradox.

RIDDLE

It comes from your sink.
It's a frosty cold drink.
It's rain streaming down
your window pane.
And your sailing boat
needs it to float.

What is it?

RIDDLE

Kids flop off their shoes, grab a book,
and nestle in my snug, embroidered lap
surrounded by my soft arms.
When the kids get up,
the cat replaces them, flipping on its back
and dozing on and off all day,
knowing I will
never move,
never stir.

What am I?

RIDDLE

We think we have
too little of it,
but no matter how
much we use of it,
we never seem to
run out of it.

We cannot stop
or grasp hold of it
or even shake
the hands on it,
though on our very
own limb it sits.

So think a minute.
What is it?

Think-through: My thoughts while writing the riddle about an armchair

First Thoughts

The book I read on riddles said that a riddle often involves a pun or a word that has a double meaning. It commonly includes a contradiction and is misleading. I'll look up some homographs, words with double meanings, on the Internet: fly, bat, batter, box, date, yard, lock. That reminds me that I often do poems about arms of chairs, legs of tables, eyes of potatoes or marbles, and so on. That would work for a riddle.

Getting Started

I'll write a riddle about a chair because it has "arms" and a "lap." I could use those aspects of a chair for the misleading part. The reader will think the poem is describing a parent or grandparent until I bring in a piece of evidence that makes it clear it's not a person. I'll say the chair "never moves, never stirs."

I'll speak in the first person and call the chair "you."

First Draft

> When I sit in your lap.
> I flop off my shoes
> pull up my legs
> and nestle into my book,
> surrounded by your soft arms.
> When I'm not there
> the cat takes my place
> on your cushion,
> sleeping all day long
> knowing you will
> never move, never stir.
>
> What are you?

Revisions/Experimenting

I read it to a friend who's a poet and she said it was confusing—it was hard to tell who was speaking, me or the chair. She said she didn't know if she was supposed to guess who "I" or "you" was.

I'll change it so the chair is speaking in the first person. If I make the chair talk about kids and cats sitting on her lap, that gets rid of the pronoun "you" and clears up the poem a lot. It'll be much easier to tell you're supposed to guess who "I "is.

My friend also said I should insert a hint when I talk about the chair's "soft lap."

I'll change it to "embroidered lap."

I could actually make this into a visual poem where the shape of the poem looks like what it's about. I could change the line breaks so it looks like the back, seat, and legs of a chair.

> Kids flop off their shoes
> and nestle in my snug
> embroidered lap
> with a favorite book
> surrounded by my strong arms.
> When they withdraw, a cat replaces them
> flipping on its back and dozing on and off
> all day, knowing I will never move
>   never   stir.

But I don't think anyone will understand. They'll be confused by why the words "never" and "stir" are so far apart. I'll change the line breaks back to the way I had them originally.

Final Draft

See page 174.

Notes on Riddle Poems

Water Riddle: This is written in couplets, and every two lines rhyme.

Armchair Riddle: See the Think-through on page 176.

Time Riddle: Even though this poem doesn't rhyme in a traditional way, it still has a rhythm and a structure to it. It sounds like it rhymes because almost every line ends with the word "it."

BIBLIOGRAPHY: RIDDLE

ELEMENTARY SCHOOL

Cerf, Bennett. *Riddles and More Riddles* (Beginner Books). New York: Random House, 1999.

Dotlich, Rebecca Kai. "Titanic," *When Riddles Come Rumbling: Poems to Ponder.* Honesdale, Pennsylvania: Boyds Mills Press, 2001, p. 28.

Franco, Betsy. *201 Thematic Riddle Poems.* New York: Scholastic, 2000.

Franco, Betsy. "Mystery Animal," "My Cousin," *Counting Our Way to the 100th Day!* New York: Margaret K. McElderry Books, 2004, pp. 29, 41.

Franco, Betsy. *Riddle Poem of the Day.* New York: Scholastic, 2005.

Lewis, J. Patrick. *Riddle-Icious*. New York: Alfred A. Knopf, 1996.

Lewis, J. Patrick. *Riddle-Lightful*. New York: Alfred A. Knopf, 1998.

Lillegard, Dee. *Hello School!* New York: Alfred A. Knopf, 2001. [could be used as riddles]

Prelutsky, Jack. "If not for the cat . . . ," *If Not for the Cat*. New York: Greenwillow, 2004.

Sierra, Judy. "Predator Riddles," *Antarctic Antics*. New York: Gulliver Books, Harcourt Brace & Company, 1998.

Silverstein, Shel. "The Toucan," *Where the Sidewalk Ends*. Harper & Row, 1974, p. 92.

Withers, Carl, compiled by. "Riddles," *A Rocket in My Pocket*. New York: Scholastic, 1948, pp. 91-97.

MIDDLE SCHOOL AND HIGH SCHOOL

Anonymous. "The beginning of eternity . . . ," *A Kick in the Head*, selected by Paul B. Janeczko. Cambridge: Candlewick Press, 2005, p. 33.

Crossley-Holland, Kevin, et. al, edited by. *The New Exeter Book of Riddles*. London: Enitharmon Press, 1999.

Tolkein, J.R. "Chapter V: Riddles in the Dark," *The Hobbit*. New York: HarperCollins, 2000.

25 SESTINA
Recommended for Grades 9-12

BACKGROUND

The sestina is most often credited to Arnaut Daniel in the late 1100s. He was a French troubadour, a traveling poet and musician. The name of the form means sixth. This is because it consists of six stanzas, or verses, with six lines in each. The six end-words of the first stanza reappear in the other stanzas according to a strict pattern. The pattern makes the sestina a rather hypnotic form of poetry to write and to read. The sestina has been written down through the ages, sometimes as a rhyming form; however, its traditional form does not include rhyme. The Italian poet Dante who wrote *The Divine Comedy* wrote poetry in this form. A famous sestina is Elizabeth Bishop's poem entitled "Sestina." (See Bibliography page 188.)

CHARACTERISTICS OF A SESTINA

- The sestina is a strict form involving 6 stanzas with 6 lines in each. The seventh stanza has 3 lines and is called the coda (ending).

- The words at the ends of the lines of the first stanza are the foundation of the poem. Those words are repeated in every stanza according to a fascinating, cyclical pattern, shown on page 180.

- The final coda (3 lines) needs to include all 6 words.

- It is easiest to start by picking 6 words and writing the first stanza. Then you can write the words at the ends of the lines according to the pattern before continuing to write.

- Poets often find that the story starts evolving once they begin writing.

- It is helpful to pick words with multiple meanings or words that can be used as different parts of speech, such as the word fly which can be a noun or a verb.

- The 6 words can come from different parts of speech: nouns, verbs, adjectives, adverbs, or conjunctions.

- The subject of the sestina is often something that can be looked at and mulled over, or even obsessed over, from different angles. For example, the poet might look at a relationship from different angles. Or, as in my sestina, I looked at a dog playing on the beach at different moments in time—the dog is constantly playing but is going from one activity to another.

- The sestina is a dynamic form because the same words keep shifting. The same words are used in different contexts.

- As the poet writes, she keeps her eyes and ears open to new insights that come out of different arrangements of the 6 words she picked.

- The 6 selected words of a sestina follow a particular pattern: in the first 6 stanzas they are the end words. In the coda, which is three lines, the words are used, with 2 of the words to each line. Traditionally, the poet uses the first 2 words in the first line of the coda and so on, but some poets just use any 2 of the 6 words for the first through third lines. Following is the pattern of the end words for a sestina:

  Stanza 1
  A
  B
  C
  D
  E
  F

  Stanza 2
  F
  A
  E
  B
  D
  C

  Stanza 3
  C
  F
  D
  A
  B
  E

  Stanza 4
  E
  C
  B
  F
  A
  D

  Stanza 5
  D
  E
  A
  C
  F
  B

Stanza 6
B
D
F
E
C
A
Coda
AB
CD
EF

Note: In my sample sestina, I mistakenly wrote 7 stanzas and a coda!

EVERYDAY PARALLELS

Someone investigating a crime collects evidence and has to keep rearranging the pieces of evidence to see what clues come out of them. The detective must solve a puzzle with no obvious answer. This process is similar to writing a sestina. The sestina is also like a dance in which you keep changing partners. You dance the same series of steps, but you keep dancing with different partners. Sometimes when people have to make a decision, they use the information they have to write out all the possible paths and outcomes and/or the pluses and minuses, in order to try to come to a conclusion. This also echoes the sestina form.

WHAT THIS FORM OFFERS

- The sestina introduces a conventional poetry form.
- The strict form will be of interest to students who like structure.
- It appeals to the logical mind.
- It involves word play.
- It can stretch vocabulary and help students see that words can be used in different ways—that words have double meanings and can be different parts of speech.
- It is challenging yet fun to write.

SESTINA

Dog Sestina

There goes the spotted dog
bounding from the car—free
to be leashless and fly
down the beach, racing
to the water and the waves
and leaping into the waiting air.

A rush of seagulls in the air
teases the yapping dog.
He watches them soar near the waves.
When they land in a cluster, he remembers he's free.
He charges and barks, racing
up to them, too late, trying hard to fly.

He forgets his desire to fly
and kicks and digs sand into the air.
He uncovers a crab that is racing
back into its hole, away from the dog.
No one yells, "No digging!" He's free
to dig, deep and hard—until he sees the waves!

Thundering, crashing, sky-green waves!
He nips at a pesky fly
and then he runs straight and free,
leaping into the waves and bounding into the air.
The waves are splashing down on the dog
and he's plunging again, then racing

down the sand, shaking and racing
away from the crazy waves,
a tired and hungry little dog.
He gobbles an old hot dog, sharing it with a sand fly.
He sniffs at the wild ocean air
and remembers that he's free.

SESTINA

A Frisbee is floating above him, free
as a white seagull, and he's racing,
and grabbing it in mid-air,
catching it again in the waves.
He can catch anything—he can fly!
He's the Frisbee-catching, never-failing super-dog.

But he can't always be so free.
Finishing one last round of racing,
he arfs good-bye to the salty air,
sashays through the calmer waves,
lunges at one last fat horse fly
and jumps in the car, a proud city dog.

Back in the city, in his dreaming, the dog is free
to dig and fly about, whipping down the sand, racing
into the waves and yipping at the salty air.

Think-through: My thoughts while writing "Dog Sestina"

First Thoughts

I know the sestina has 6 key words.

It might be easiest to start with mostly nouns.

I'd like to pick some words that have double meanings so I can use them in different ways. I remember this from Elizabeth Bishop's "Sestina." Glad I read that before starting.

I'd better choose a topic, something I know a lot about because the sestina has 6 stanzas and a coda (ending), and each one needs to say something different.

I've been writing poems about dogs lately so maybe I can use dogs somehow.

Dogs are happiest at the park running around, or better yet, at the beach.

I've seen lots of dogs at the beach in the summer.

That's it.

Getting Started

I'll brainstorm some possible things to write about dogs at the beach and then pick 6 words.

I could write about:
>dogs playing in the waves
>digging up the sand
>eating scraps
>bounding in the waves
>chasing birds
>playing with a ball

Some possible words:
>*dog*
>*free* has two meanings
>*sand*
>*waves* has two meanings
>*air*
>*race* can be a noun or verb
>*ball*
>*fly* has two meanings

I'm going to use a variety of words: *waves, race, fly, free, air,* and *dog.*

I've got to write the first stanza to figure out the order of the words.
>There goes the dog
>bounding from the car, free
>to be leashless and fly
>down the beach, racing
>to the water, and waves
>and jumping in the air.

I changed "race" to "racing." Now I'm going to map it out like a chart and put the end words in.

A	dog
B	free
C	fly
D	racing
E	waves
F	air

F	air
A	dog
E	waves
B	free
D	racing
C	fly

C	fly
F	air
D	racing
A	dog
B	free
E	waves

E	waves
C	fly
B	free
F	air
A	dog
D	racing

D	racing
E	waves
A	dog
C	fly
F	air
B	free

B	free
D	racing
F	air
E	waves
C	fly
A	dog

AB	dog, free
CD	fly, racing
EF	waves, air

185

First Draft

There goes the dog
bounding from the car, free
to be leashless and fly
down the beach, racing
to the water, and waves
and jumping in the air.

A swoosh of seagulls in the air
teases the yipping dog
He watches them soar over the waves.
When they land in a cluster, he's free.
He charges and yips, racing and racing.
When they take off, he tries to fly.

He forgets his desire to fly
and kicks and digs sand into the air.
A crab peeks out and is racing
back into his house, away from the dog.
No one stops his digging, he's free
to dig as much as he wants—until he sees the waves!

Thundering, crashing, sky-green waves!
The dog nips at a pesty fly
and then runs free,
leaping and bounding into the air.
The waves crash on the dog
and he's plunging and racing

down the sand, wet and racing
away from the pounding waves,
a tired and hungry little dog,
He gobbles at his treat, sharing it with a fly.
He sniffs at the wild ocean air
and remembers that he's free.

A Frisbee is floating above him, free
as a bird, and he's racing,
and grabs it in mid-air,
He catches it again in the waves.
He can catch anything—he can fly!
He's a super, Frisbee-catching dog.

But the dog cannot always be so free.
He finishes one last round of racing,
he yips good-bye to the salty air,
he tiptoes through the calmer waves,
nips at one last fly
He jumps in the car, he's a city dog.

[Now I have to put together all the words in the final three lines.

I'll work with the idea that he's a city dog.]

> In the city, the dog is content but he's not so free
> to fly about, racing, racing
> with the thundering waves and yipping at the air.

Revising/Experimenting

This was easier than I thought because I picked a topic that was so rich—a dog at the beach. And with the end words already written in, I could just fashion the story as I went along. It was fun and it flowed.

Now, I'd better look at my word choices.
- "leaping in the air" instead of "jumping in the air"
- I don't want to overuse "yips." I'll use "bark," "yip," "arf" throughout.
- "pesky fly" instead of "pesty fly"
- "shaking and racing away from the crazy waves" is better than "wet and racing away from the pounding waves" because it's a better image, and I don't want the waves to seem unfriendly and dangerous.
- The dog doesn't "tiptoe" through the waves, he "sashays" through the waves.
- I want to emphasize that he's a city dog so I can make the last three lines a surprise when he's back in the city. I'll say, "a proud city dog" right before the last three lines.

I'll put details in where I've been general.
- "spotted dog" instead of "dog"
- "No one yells, 'No digging!'" instead of "No one stops his digging."
- "He's free to dig deep and hard" is better than "He's free to dig as much as he wants." The words are better, and the first phrase had too many little, uninteresting words.
- "sand fly" and "fat horse fly" are better than "fly."
- "Free as a bird" is a cliché; "free as a white seagull" is much better.

I'll take out unnecessary words.
- "racing to the water and waves" instead of "racing to the water and the waves"

I'll clarify the images and the tone/mood:
- I'll change "He races up to the seagulls, too late, and tries to fly." to "He charges and barks, racing/up to them, too late, trying hard to fly."
- "A crab peeks out" is a better image than "He uncovers a crab . . ."
- In the last stanza, "In the city, the dog is content but he's not free/to fly about, racing," "racing" is kind of negative and not specific enough. I'll make it about what he can do—he can dream about the beach—and I'll make it more specific, too:

> "Back in the city, in his dreams, the dog is free
> to dig and fly about, whipping down the sand, racing
> into the waves and yipping at the salty air."

One last look:
I made 7 stanzas and a coda instead of 6 stanzas and a coda! I guess I'll just leave in the stanza about the Frisbee, but next time I'll count my stanzas more carefully.

Final Draft

See pages 182-183.

BIBLIOGRAPHY: SESTINA

MIDDLE SCHOOL AND HIGH SCHOOL

Bishop, Elizabeth. "Sestina." Retrieved October 4, 2004 from **http://www.sccs.swarthmore.edu/users/03/ahead/sestina.html**.

Hecht, Anthony. "The Book of Yolek," *The Making of a Poem,* edited by Mark Strand and Eavan Boland. New York: W.W. Norton, 2000, p. 37-38.

Koertge, Ron. "And a Half Order of Sestina, Please," *Shakespeare Bats Cleanup.* Cambridge: Candlewick Press, 2003, p. 50.

Williams, Miller. "The Shrinking Lonesome Sestina," *The Making of a Poem,* edited by Mark Strand and Eavan Boland. New York: W.W. Norton, 2000, p. 38-39.

26 SONNET
Recommended for Grades 7-12

BACKGROUND

An Italian poet Giacomo da Lentino is often credited with creating the sonnet, as we know it, in 1200 A.D. In Italian, sonnet means "little sound or song." Many people are familiar with Shakespeare's sonnets, including the line, "Shall I compare thee to a summer's day?" One of the most famous sonnets is by Elizabeth Barrett Browning and starts: "How do I love thee? Let me count the ways . . ." Traditionally, sonnets are 14-line poems about love and/or a large philosophical question, but modern poets have written sonnets about many other subjects, including spiders and atomic bomb testing.

CHARACTERISTICS OF A SONNET

- The sonnet has 14 lines.
- In the Petrarchan sonnet, the first 8 lines develop an idea. In the last 6 lines, the poet draws some conclusions about the idea or tells how she or he feels about the idea. There is a shift in thinking from the first 8 lines to the last 6 lines.
- In the Shakespearean and Spenserian sonnets, there is a rhyming couplet (two lines) at the end, the poet develops the idea over 12 lines and gradually comes to some final conclusion in the last two lines.
- The traditional rhythm, or meter, for a sonnet is iambic pentameter, which is 5 iambs (da DA). (See *beat* and *rhythm* in Glossary.)
  da DA, da DA, da DA, da DA, da DA
- For the Petrarchan sonnet, which is divided into 8 lines and 6 lines, the rhyme scheme is often ABBA ABBA CDECDE. (See *rhyme scheme* in Glossary.)
- The rhyme scheme of the Shakespearean sonnet is ABAB CDCD, EFEF GG. The first 8 lines are divided into two 4-line stanzas called quatrains. The next 6 lines are divided into a 4-line stanza and a couplet.
- The Spenserian sonnet has the following rhyme scheme: ABAB BCBC CDCD EE
- Traditionally, the subject is love, but sonnets can be about anything.
- The subject of love is often used as a pretext for writing about some philosophical question, such as, "Can true love last?"
- The language is often heightened, and the sonnet is usually quite emotional.
- In a mirror sonnet, the poem is divided into 7 lines and 7 lines. The second 7 lines are a mirror image of the first 7 lines, with some variation.

EVERYDAY PARALLELS

Love letters, notes professing love, and e-mails about love are parallel to a sonnet in everyday life. Love songs are also similar to sonnets.

WHAT THIS FORM OFFERS

- The sonnet introduces a conventional poetry form.
- The rhythm is an easy one to write, and it doesn't need to be followed strictly. Neither does the rhyme scheme.
- The structure is challenging, but it can be fun if the restrictions are loosened as much as needed. The only necessary restriction is that the sonnet be 14 lines.
- Writing the sonnet teaches students to present a hypothesis and come to a conclusion.
- It offers students an opportunity to heighten their language, and to write in a style that is very emotional.

SONNET

Sonnet

When first we met one day in algebra,
you equaled that sonnet of "a summer's day."
Your short-cropped hair with streaks of plum,
Your artistry showing in multiple ways.
Complex equations, only, give a clue
how, exponentially, our feelings spread
so quickly that I had no need of proof
nor need to gauge what lay ahead.
Our love seemed infinite as autumn's wind
till fears of closeness surfaced to resolve.
Illusions crushed, transformed to winter's chill,
dividing us in ways so hard to solve.
But as one plus one will always equal two,
we balanced our fragile equation anew.

Mirror Sonnet

The file is blank, the desktop's royal blue.
I'll whip off this sonnet—just heard that it's due.
Or should I write about my inner doubts,
about pretending that I'm someone that I'm not.
Each morning I delete my real self
and write a script for everyone to see.
That character has little to do with me.

The character has little to do with me
when I follow a script for everyone to see.
Tonight, for once, I won't delete myself,
I won't pretend that I am someone else.
I'll write about my strange and inner doubts
inside this mirror sonnet that is due
. . . but then I'll turn in one that isn't true.

First Thoughts

I think I'll do a mirror sonnet as one of the sonnets because Anthony Kirkland wrote one in the anthology I compiled entitled *You Hear Me? poems and writing by teenage boys,* and it was powerful. I sense that some students will probably relate to this form better than a traditional sonnet. In this form the first 7 lines are reversed in the second stanza.

I had a discussion with a friend about how kids sometimes abandon their dreams in a tough economy, and it's a shame because it's easiest to take risks when you're young and just starting out. I am a writer and I try to encourage students to be artists if that's their passion. I explain that they have to be creative about making a living, and that I do make a living as a writer.

Getting Started

Since my oldest son is a successful actor, I'll choose acting as the dream that the narrator is deciding whether to pursue. I won't use any of my son's true attitudes or feelings in this poem.

I'll start by reading some samples of sonnets to pick up the rhythm and the rhyme scheme.

Now I need to think about the mirror sonnet. I need 7 lines in the first stanza and 7 lines in the last stanza. What I'll be doing is reversing the first stanza, with some variations, to create the second stanza.

As I'm writing, every once in a while, I'll test what it would say if the lines were written in reverse.

In the second stanza I'll change some words to make the logic flow, so the second stanza is a slight variation of the first.

I think I'll have a rhyme scheme of AABB CDD, DDC BBAA.

Seventh Draft

I'm including the seventh draft because I ended up completely changing this and I want to show what happened.

Acting?

Will I try to be an actor, though I'm scared?
The hunger's fierce, so is the talent there?
Auditions where emotions must be bared,
like market meat exposed in open air!
Rejection—can I stand to be its prey?
To get a break seems distant, needle-thin,
but buckling to my dragons seems so grim.

Buckling to my dragons seems so grim,
and breaks seem distant, needle-thin.
Rejection—I can't stand to be its prey,
like market meat exposed in open air.
Auditions where emotions must be bared
make hunger fierce—the talent will be there.
I'll try to be an actor though I'm scared.

Revisions/Experimenting

In reading it over, I have references to meat markets, jungles and dragons. I never focused on one metaphor/comparison that I could extend throughout the poem. I think that's called mixed metaphors.

A sonnet is usually about emotions, not necessarily a story or a logical choice like deciding on a career path, or if it is, the emotions are stressed, or there's some universal question that's being pondered.

I don't know enough about acting to pull this off, to come up with a theme or question that will ring true. I'm going to scratch this and start over. I learned a lot about the structure from doing this mirror sonnet, though.

I'll do something related, but about writing this time, since I'm a writer. In my new poem, I'll focus on the metaphor of writing on the computer, with its blank page and deletions. The theme will be about whether to reveal your inner feelings in a poem, to be vulnerable or not. Ironically, I love to anthologize personal poems by teenagers and young adults but it's hard for me to be vulnerable in my own writing. Although, lately, I've been giving it a try.

New Try

This is about the fifteenth draft!

Mirror Sonnet

The file is blank, the desktop's royal blue.
I'll whip off this sonnet—just heard that it's due.
Or should I write about my inner doubts,
about pretending that I'm someone else.
Each morning I delete my real self
and write a script for everyone to see.
That character has little to do with me.

The character has little to do with me
when I follow a script for everyone to see.
Tonight, for once, I won't delete myself,
I won't pretend that I am someone else.
I'll write about my strange and inner doubts
inside this mirror sonnet that is due
. . . but then I'll turn in one that isn't true.

Final Draft

See page 191.

Notes on Poems

Sonnet: I spent a lot of time putting algebraic/mathematical and seasonal references in this sonnet to make it more than just a poem about a relationship—to add texture to the poem. I like that you can't tell if it's a boy talking about a girl, a girl talking about a boy, a pair of boys, or a pair of girls. I wrote the poem rhyming every other line in each quatrain at first (ABCB, DEFE, GHIH, JJ) but then I made it more like a Shakespearean sonnet (ABAB, CDCD, EFEF, GG). I introduced the situation in the first 8 lines and gradually came to a conclusion in the last quatrain (4 lines) and the final couplet (2 lines). I wrote at least 20 drafts of this sonnet.

Mirror Sonnet: See Think-through on page 192.

BIBLIOGRAPHY: SONNET

ELEMENTARY SCHOOL

McNaughton, Colin. "The Lady in Love," *Making Friends with Frankenstein*. Cambridge: Candlewick Press, 1994, p. 40. [sonnet-like]

ALL LEVELS

Roberts, Georgia Dunston. "The Wolf," *Talking Like the Rain,* selected by X.J. Kennedy and Dorothy M. Kennedy. New York: Little, Brown and Company, 1992, p. 58.

MIDDLE SCHOOL AND HIGH SCHOOL

Bishop, Elizabeth. "Sonnet," *Elizabeth Bishop, The Complete Poems 1927-1979*. New York: Farrar, Straus and Giroux, 1983, p. 214.

Blanchard, Kyle. "Sleep," *You Hear Me? poems and writing by teenage boys,* edited by Betsy Franco. Cambridge: Candlewick Press, 2000, p. 31.

Browning, Elizabeth Barrett. "How do I love thee? . . . " *Elizabeth Barrett Browning (1806-1861)*. Retrieved October 4, 2004 from **http://www.sonnets.org/brownine.htm#043.**

Chappell, Seth. "Does My Mother Look Like This?," *You Hear Me? poems and writing by teenage boys*, edited by Betsy Franco. Cambridge: Candlewick Press, 2000, p.48.

Kirkland, Anthony E.W. "Bumming Through Pittsburgh? Maybe Not." *You Hear Me? poems and writing by teenage boys,* edited by Betsy Franco. Cambridge: Candlewick Press, 2000, p. 65. [mirror sonnet]

Koertge, Ron. "In That Book of Dad's I Borrowed," *Shakespeare Bats Cleanup*. Cambridge: Candlewick Press, 2003, p. 15.

Lewis, J. Patrick. "Letter to Galileo from His Daughter, Sister Maria Celeste," *Galileo's Universe*. Mankato, Minnesota: Creative Editions, 2005.

Little Light, Byron "Dirk." "My Love," *Night Is Gone, Day Is Still Coming, stories and poems by American Indian teenagers and young adults,* edited by Betsy Franco. Cambridge: Candlewick Press, 2003, p. 113.

Rosaldo, Renato. "Secret Lovers," *Prayer to Spider Woman/Rezo a la mujer araña*. Saltillo, Coahuila, Mexico: Instituto Coahuilense de Cultura, 2003, pp. 90-91.

Shakespeare, William. "Sonnet Number Twelve," *A Kick in the Head,* selected by Paul B. Janeczko. Cambridge: Candlewick Press, 2005, p. 28.

Shakespeare, William. "Shall I compare thee to a summer's day?," *William Shakespeare (1564-1616)*. Retrieved October 8, 2004 from **http://www.sonnets.org/shakespeare.htm#018.**

Shakespeare, William. "Sonnet 18," "Sonnet 116," "Sonnet 29," *William Shakespeare Poetry for Young People,* edited by David Scott Kastan and Marina Kastan. New York: Sterling, 2000.

Sonnet Central. Retrieved October 8, 2004 from **http://www.sonnets.org/.**

Wayland, April Halprin. "My Version of William Shakespeare's Sonnet Number Twelve," *A Kick in the Head,* selected by Paul B. Janeczko. Cambridge: Candlewick Press, 2005, p. 29.

27 VISUAL POETRY
Recommended for Grades K-12

BACKGROUND

Visual poems have taken many forms over the years, as far back as the Greeks. Many of the first poems were called "shape poems," Because the shape of the poem reflected its subject matter. In the 1600s, George Hebert wrote a poem called "Easter Wings" where the text is in the shape of angel wings. In the early 1900s, surrealist poet Guillaume Apollinaire wrote poems in the shape of falling rain, a valentine, and more. He called them calligrams. About 60 years later, a German poet Reinhard Döhl wrote a famous poem in the shape of an apple with the word "apfel" written over and over inside the shape, except for one spot that says "wurm." By that time, poets used the term "concrete poetry" to refer to this very literal kind of visual poem.

Other types of visual poetry have developed over the years, in which the poet plays with the placement of the text, the white space, individual letters of words, the font, and/or the color of the text to reflect visually the meaning or action of the poem. Some critics disparage visual poetry as just a clever trick, but it has become more widely accepted as a conventional form.

CHARACTERISTICS OF A VISUAL POEM

- Visual poetry combines some visual element with the words of the poem.
- The poem works on many levels: on a meaning level, on a sound level (the way the words sound), and on a graphic/visual level.
- A visual poem is rarely left-justified on the page. It is often laid out in an unusual way.
- Sometimes the poem is difficult to read aloud. Sometimes it is just meant to be viewed and read to yourself.
- In visual poems called "concrete poems," the poem is in the shape of the subject of the poem.
- In other visual poems, the layout on the page reflects the action described in the poem. For example, a poem about sledding could swoop down the page.
- The page layout and the text can "act out" the theme of the poem or the meaning of the words. For example, in a poem about a fight, the words could be overlapping, upside-down and sideways.
- The text can be manipulated so that the print—size, font, color, placement, space, punctuation—becomes an integral part of the poem. For example, in a poem about a messy room, the names of clothing and personal items

could be jumbled up together so that they were a bit challenging to read.
- The length and nature of the poem can vary widely: It can read like a rhymed or free verse poem or it can involve just a few words that interact. For example, in a minimalist visual poem, a word such as balance or strength could be written in a way that contradicts the meaning of the word itself. Or the words feeling alone could be written with the letter *l* of alone elongated to represent a person feeling alone even in a crowd.

EVERYDAY PARALLELS

In elementary school, children often create books in the shape of the subject they're writing about—an apple, a heart. Or when children act out a poem or illustrate it, they are approaching the concept of visual poetry. Graffitti comes close, as well as catalogs, posters, and advertisements. Posters of movies or rock groups sometimes have poetic text, or words written in a graphic way.

WHAT THIS FORM OFFERS

- Visual poetry introduces a conventional poetry form.
- It is very effective with visual learners.
- It integrates text and graphic elements.
- It is fun to write. Students who think they dislike poetry writing can suddenly find themselves having a good time.
- It encourages a high degree of creativity and cleverness.

VISUAL POETRY

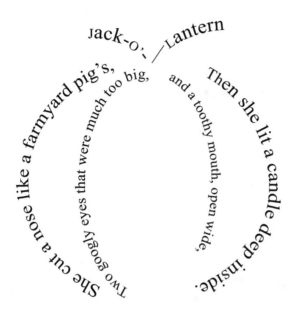

Jack-o'-Lantern

She cut a nose like a farmyard pig's,
Two googly eyes that were much too big,
and a toothy mouth, open wide,
Then she lit a candle deep inside.

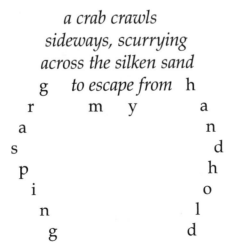

a crab crawls
sideways, scurrying
across the silken sand
g   *to escape from*   h
r   m   y   a
a   n
s   d
p   h
i   o
n   l
g   d

VISUAL POETRY

body surfing through my life

catching the spray-crested wave and riding it—no doubts, just momentum all the way to shore

treading
treading
treading
treading

VISUAL POETRY

Two Friends Fighting
with Words

they tease

they taunt

bite

belittle

hurl insults

smash feelings

shout

bark

clash

howl

take some space

sort of apologize

& get back to goofing around

licking their wounds

though both are still

Think-through: My thoughts while writing the visual poem about a crab

First Thoughts

I've tried some different kinds of visual poems; I'll think about what kind of visual poem is left to do:

I have a visual poem about body surfing where the motion of the surfer is reflected in the layout of the poem.

I have a visual poem about a pumpkin in which the lines of the poem are written on the lines of the pumpkin.

I have a poem in which the words describe an argument and the placement of the text on the page reflects the fight.

But I haven't written a visual poem in which the words form a solid object—the object I'm talking about in the poem.

I could write about a frog or a grasshopper but I've done that before. What animals have something strange or distinctive about them that's visual? Octopus, crab, anteater, flying birds, roly-poly bug.

I think I'll try a crab because I've seen them at the beach, and my kids used to try to dig them up and grab them.

Getting Started

I'll write the poem in the shape of a crab.

It will be a crab trying to get away from a child.

I'll make the lines of the poem that describe the kid's grasping hands look like the claws of the crab.

First I'll write it, sort of in the shape of a crab.

This part will be the body:

a crab
walks sideways
to scurry across
the sand
away

This part will be the claws:

from our
grasping hands

First Draft

Now I'll put it sideways and put in the claws.

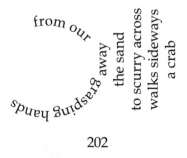

202

Revising/Experimenting

It needs to have a fatter body and shorter claws.

I'll lengthen the lines and increase the drama as well.

I'll put fewer words on the claws.

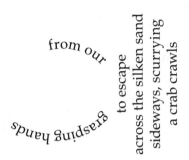

I need to think about this visually—the claws should be on either side of the body.

Should the crab be sideways or not? It's too hard to read this way.

It's easier to read if it's not sideways. I'll turn it around so people will read left to right. That will make it look like the crab is moving sideways, which is how crabs move.

I'll change it to "my grasping hands" instead of "from our grasping hands." The word "my" has two letters and I can make the *m* and *y* look like the crab's eyes.

I'll change "grasping hands" to "grasping handhold" to make the claws the same length.

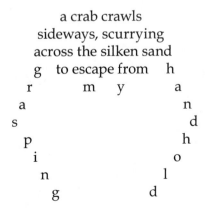

I think it's okay that the claws are so long. They represent the claws and the narrator's hands grabbing for the crab.

I'll try formatting the body of the crab in italics so it looks like it's moving across the sand.

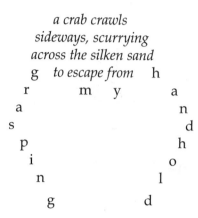

I'll try different fonts. I sort of like Verdana, bodoni bold, but I think I'll go back to Times, 18 point type.

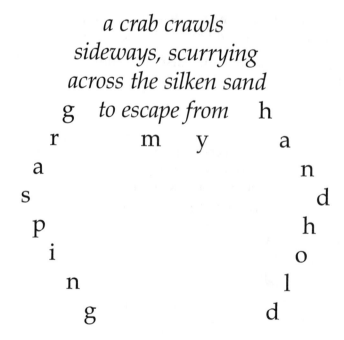

I'll go back to 14 point type.

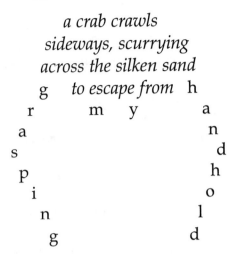

a crab crawls
sideways, scurrying
across the silken sand
g   *to escape from*   h
  r   m   y   a
  a   n
    s   d
    p   h
      i   o
      n   l
        g   d

Final Draft

See page 199.

Notes on Poems

Jack-O'-Lantern: Although "pig" and "big" are commonly rhymed and I try to avoid easy rhymes, at least I made the images unusual. In the last line, I changed the tone to a more contemplative tone.

Crab: See Think-through on page 202.

body surfing through my life: I wanted the poem to show the motion, the action of body surfing but also to reflect what it can be like in life to "ride out" or "go with" an opportunity that comes your way.

Two Friends Fighting with Words: I wanted the words at all different angles all over the page to reflect what a fight feels like.

BIBLIOGRAPHY: VISUAL POETRY

ELEMENTARY SCHOOL

Burg, Brad. *Outside the Lines.* G.P. Putnam's Sons, 2002.

Cassedy, Sylvia. "Elevator," *The 20th Century Children's Poetry Treasury,* selected by Jack Prelutsky. New York: Alfred A. Knopf, 1999, p. 42.

Creech, Sharon. "My Yellow Dog, by Jack" *Love That Dog.* New York: Joanna Cotler Books/HarperCollins, 2001, p. 37.

Dotlich, Rebecca Kai. "Porcupine," *Hoofbeats, Claws & Rippled Fins: Creature Poems.* New York: HarperCollins, 2002, p. 26.

Fatchen, Max. "Shakes and Ladders," *The 20th Century Children's Poetry Treasury* selected by Jack Prelutsky. New York: Alfred A. Knopf, 1999, p. 43.

Florian, Douglas. "The Gecko," "The Python," "The Polliwogs," *lizards, frogs, and polliwogs*. New York: Harcourt, 2001, p. 10, 25, 30.

Florian, Douglas. "The Salmon," *The 20th Century Children's Poetry Treasury*, selected by Jack Prelutsky. New York: Alfred A. Knopf, 1999, p. 42.

George, Emily. "To Start a Day Aliona's Way," *Pocket Poems*, selected by Bobbi Katz. New York: Dutton, 2004, p. 2.

George, Kristine O'Connell. "Egg," *The 20th Century Children's Poetry Treasury*, selected by Jack Prelutsky. New York: Alfred A. Knopf, 1999, p. 43.

George, Kristine O'Connell. "Morning Nap," *Little Dog Poems*. New York: Clarion Books, 1999, p. 11.

George, Kristine O'Connell. "Tree's Place," *Old Elm Speaks*. New York: Clarion, 1998, p. 25.

Hoberman, Mary Ann. "Giraffes," *Eric Carle's Animals Animals*. New York: Philomel Books, 1989, p. 48.

Lewis, J. Patrick. "Autograph Verse," *The Bookworm's Feast*. New York: Dial Books, 1999.

Lewis, J. Patrick. *Doodle Dandies*. New York: Atheneum, 1998.

Prelutsky, Jack. "I Was Walking in a Circle," "A Triangle Tale," *A Pizza the Size of the Sun*. New York: Greenwillow, 1996, pp. 23, 60.

Prelutsky, Jack. "I Was Walking in a Circle," *The 20th Century Children's Poetry Treasury*, selected by Jack Prelutsky. New York: Alfred A. Knopf, 1999, p. 42.

Rigg, S.C. "The Apple," *Love That Dog* by Sharon Creech. Joanna Cotler Books/HarperCollins, 2001.

Singer, Marilyn. "There Once Was a Golden Retriever," *It's Hard to Read a Map with a Beagle on Your Lap*. New York: Henry Holt, 1993.

West, Colin. "Rolling Down the Hill," *The 20th Century Children's Poetry Treasury*, selected by Jack Prelutsky. New York: Alfred A. Knopf, 1999, p. 43.

ALL LEVELS

Janeczko, Paul B. *A Poke in the I*. Cambridge: Candlewick Press, 2001.

Kulling, Monica. "Amelia Cramped," *A Kick in the Head*, selected by Paul B. Janeczko. Cambridge: Candlewick Press, 2005, p. 38.

Graham, Joan Branfield. "A Kick in the Head," *A Kick in the Head*, selected by Paul B. Janeczko. Cambridge: Candlewick Press, 2005, p. 39.

MIDDLE SCHOOL AND HIGH SCHOOL

aND' mIEKAL, edited by. *Spidertangle*. Dreamtime Village, WI: Xexoxial Editions, 2002. E-mail dtv@mwt.net. XEXOXIAL EDITIONS, LaFarge, WI. http://www.xeroxial.org. [avant-garde visual poems]

Apollinaire, Guillaume. *Calligrams*. Greensboro, North Carolina: Unicorn Press, 1973.

Apollinaire, Guillaume. "Horse (Homme)," *Paris in the 20s Poetry*. Retrieved September 28, 2004 from **http://www.bbc.co.uk/music/features/paris/poetry.shtml.**

Carroll, Lewis. "Chapter III: A Caucus Race and A Long Tale," *Alice's Adventures in Wonderland*. [See visual poem of mouse tail] cummings, e.e. "1(a le af f all . . .," retrieved February 14, 2005 from **http.//www.angelfire.com/weird2/emilyrocks/eecummings.html.**

cummings, e.e. "r-p-o-p-h-e-s-s-a-g-r," *poets.org*. Retrieved August 12, 2005 from **http://www.poets.org/viewmedia.php/prmMID/15402.**

Glenn, Mel. "Esther Torres," "Morton Potter," "Brad McCall," *The Taking of Room 114*. New York: Lodestar Books, Dutton, 1997, pp. 68, 102, 124-128.

Glenn, Mel. "Library Fun," "Library Fun II," "metronome," *Split Image*. New York: HarperCollins, 2000, pp. 58, 80, 103.

Glenn, Mel. "Stereotype I," "Brian Paxell," *Foreign Exchange*. New York: Morrow Junior Books, 1999, pp. 40, 93.

Grumman, Bob. *Xerolage30, a selection of visual poems*. Dreamtime Village, WI: Xexoxial Editions, 2002. E-mail dtv@mwt.net. XEXOXIAL EDITIONS, LaFarge, WI, **http://www.xeroxial.org.** [avant-garde visual poems]

Hennessy, Neil. "Basho's Frogger," "vOw(h)e(e)ls (for John Riddell)," "vOw(h)e(e)ls 2." Retrieved October 1, 2004 from **http://www.ubu.com/contemp/hennessy/hennessy.html.** [avant-garde poetry]

Hollander, John. "Swan and Shadow," *Richard Grantham*. Retrieved September 28, 2004 from **http://www.anagrammy.com/literary/rg/poems-rg18.html.**

Mountain, Marlene. "frog . . .," "peacock," "coyote . . .," "raindrop," "sn wfl k s," *The Haiku Anthology*, edited by Cor Van Den Heuvel. New York: Simon & Schuster, 1986, pp. 156, 163-164.

Stefans, Brian Kim. "the dreamlife of letters," *the dreamlife of letters*. retrieved August 12, 2005 from **http://www.ubu.com/contemp/stefans/dream/index.html.** [avantgarde poetry]

FINAL THOUGHTS

I wrote this book so that teachers will enjoy teaching poetry, so that teachers will be able to demonstrate poetry writing for their students, so that teachers and students will find out that they are poets, and so that students will feel more comfortable in their own skins by writing poetry regularly in the classroom.

I invite you to make this book your own. Add your students' poems and your own poems to the samples you use to teach. Add books to the bibliographies. Add poetry forms to the list of forms you teach. Make poetry something you can't wait to teach and that students can't wait to learn!

POET BIOGRAPHIES

These poets have been quoted throughout the book and their work appears in the bibliographies.

Jessie Childress, who graduated from the School of Journalism at the University of Montana in 2003, is currently working as the copy editor at a weekly alternative newspaper. She still reads and writes poetry, and it remains her favorite form of the written word. Richard Hugo and Wallace Stevens are among her best-loved poets. Her poetry can be found in *Things I Have to Tell You, poems and writing by teenage girls.*

Maria Damon teaches poetry and poetics at the University of Minnesota. She is the author of *The Dark End of the Street: Margins in American Vanguard Poetry,* and co-author (with Betsy Franco) of *The Secret Life of Words,* and (with mIEKAL aND), of *Literature Nation* and other book-length poems.

Rebecca Kai Dotlich is a poet and picture book author whose poetry has appeared in numerous magazines, anthologies and textbooks. *Lemonade Sun and Other Summer Poems* was selected as an IRA-CBC Children's Choice Award, and *Away We Go!* earned an Oppenheim Toy Portfolio Gold award and was chosen for Best Book for Babies top 10 list. She is a frequent speaker at conferences and teaches writing workshops to children and adults. In addition, she has been a contributing columnist for *Teaching K-8* magazine.

Playing in recorder consorts and string quartets led **Paul Fleischman** to his poems for multiple voices. Many of his prose books are likewise designed for performance, from the picture book *Lost!* to the young adult novels *Seek* and *Mind's Eye* to his madcap play, *Zap.* You can learn more about the author at www.paulfleischman.net.

Mahogany Foster is a performance poet, MC, musician and playwright, and gives poetry workshops at high schools. Her one-woman show *The Foster Child* has been presented for Bay Area and New York City audiences. Mahogany also co-produced a hip-hop album under the name Mo'Betta. Her poetry is published in *Things I Have to Tell You, poems and writing by teenage girls.*

Mel Glenn, the author of 12 Young Adult books, among them *Split Image* and *Who Killed Mr. Chippendale?,* retired in 2001 after teaching high school English for 34 years in the New York City Public School System, 31 years at his alma mater, Abraham Lincoln High School in Brooklyn. He now writes and travels across the country speaking to children and adults at libraries, schools and conferences. His techie sons made him a website at www. melglenn.com.

Poet/critic **Bob Grumman** writes a regular column about poetry for *Small Press Review*. Although best known as a poet for his hybrid of haiku and mathematics, the "mathemaku," he also composes visual and traditional poetry. He lives with his cat, Shirley, in Port Charlotte, Florida, where he scratches out a living as a high school substitute teacher.

Steve Healey's first book of poetry, *Earthling,* was published by Coffee House Press in 2004. He lives in Minneapolis, where he's working on a Ph.D. in English literature at the University of Minnesota, and teaching writing to prisoners in several Minnesota Correctional Facilities.

Lee Bennett Hopkins is a distinguished poet, writer, and anthologist. His awards and honors include the University of Southern Mississippi Medallion for "lasting contributions to children's literature," the Keystone State Author of the Year Award, four ALA Notable Book Awards, the Christopher Award, and a Golden Kite Honor Award. His books include *My America, Good Books, Good Times!, Wonderful Words,* and *Days to Celebrate.*

Until she became a bona fide author with the publication of her first book, **Joy Hulme** described herself as a "part-time everything and a full-time nothing." She claims her specialty is non-fiction in poetry because her picture books, such as *Sea Squares, Sea Sums,* and *Wild Fibonacci,* contain a great deal of accurate animal information. But she also enjoys whimsy and word play, so her work is often a combination of both. She lives in Monte Sereno, California.

Paul B. Janeczko taught high school English for 22 years before leaving the classroom to spend more time writing and working with children as a visiting poet. He has published over 40 books, including 4 collections of his own poems and 25 poetry anthologies. He lives in western Maine.

Stephan Johnson is a twenty-three year old poet from Detroit, Michigan. He has been involved in poetry and creative writing through his involvement in the InsideOut Literary Arts Project. He was a student in the program in his high school years, and now he is teaching poetry and creative writing to sixth, seventh, and eighth graders through the program. His poems can be found in *You Hear Me? poems and writing by teenage boys.*

Bobbi Katz grew up when the radio brought jazz tunes and rhyming lyrics right into the living room, and that's when she fell in love with words and rhythm. The romance has lasted. She's been a fashion editor, a writer for *The Cousteau Almanac,* and the author of many books for young people, especially poetry collections. She hopes that the 65 first-person poems she wrote for *We the People* help history come alive for kids.

Brian Laidlaw recently graduated from Stanford University, where he studied poetry. He is also a folk and blues guitarist and lyricist, with songs that take shape from of his poems. Brian's first album, *Quarter-Life,* juxtaposes his writing and music in a combination book/CD. His heart permanently resides in the Sierra Nevada mountains. See www.brianlaidlaw.com.

J. Patrick Lewis was an economics professor on the midland moors of Ohio for thirty years before the gods had him reincarnated as a children's poet. After his three children and poetry, his greatest love is Russia, which he has visited eleven times. He has published thirty-nine books to date.

Kris Aro McLeod is an illustrator, writer, and art teacher. She has worked as an Artist in Residence and as a California Poet in the Schools. Her poetry can be found in children's poetry anthologies, including Lee Bennett Hopkin's *My America*, in magazines, and on audio recordings. She lives in Northern California with her husband and their two children.

Renato Rosaldo received an American Book Award, 2004, for his bilingual (Spanish-English) collection of poems, *Prayer to Spider Woman/Rezo a la mujer araña*. In 2000 he was awarded first prize for excellence in poetry by *El Andar* magazine. As a cultural anthropologist at New York University, he is the author of *Culture and Truth*.

Rene Ruiz wrote poetry as a participant in a series of drop-in writing workshops sponsored by Writers in the Schools (WITS) in Houston, Texas at Davis High School. His poem "He Shaved His Head" appears in *You Hear Me? poems and writing by teenage boys.*

Marilyn Singer is the author of over seventy children's books, including fifteen poetry collections. Her most recent collections are *Creature Carnival* (Hyperion) and *Central Heating: Poems About Fire and Warmth* (Knopf). She lives in Brooklyn, New York and Washington, Connecticut, with her husband and a number of pets.

Gary Soto is the author of twenty-five books for adults and young readers. He serves as Young People's Ambassador for both California Rural Legal Assistance (CRLA) and the United Farm Workers of America (UFW).

Miriam Stone is the author of *At the End of Words: A Daughter's Memoir,* winner of the 2004 International Reading Association Children's Book Award in Young Adult Nonfiction. Her poetry has also been published in Betsy Franco's anthology *Things I Have to Tell You: poems and writing by teenage girls.* A graduate of the Undergraduate Creative Writing Program at Columbia University, Stone lives in Brooklyn, where she works as a writer and editor and is completing her first novel.

Katie McAllaster Weaver's poems have been featured in *Highlights, Cricket, Ladybug,* and *Cicada.* Others have been included in Scholastic and Milkweed anthologies as well as current and future Lee Bennett Hopkins' collections. Picture books include *Bill in a China Shop* (Bloomsbury). Forthcoming Easy Reader Series: *Pete & Joe* (Simon & Schuster 2008).

Sarah Wilson is the author and sometimes illustrator of 27 books for children. They include a poetry collection, *June is a Tune That Jumps on a Stair;* a narrative poem in *Three in a Balloon,* and rhyming verse in *Garage Song, Good Zap, Little Grog* and most recently *Love and Kisses.* She lives with her family in Northern California.

Thomas Yeahpau hails from the Kiowa Nation out of Anadarko, Oklahoma. He is currently a student at Haskell Indian Nations University, again. When he's not shooting a short film, acting in a play, producing music, or writing a novel, he's writing poetry. He is the author of *The X-Indian Chronicles: The Book of Mausape* (2006) and his poetry appears in *Night Is Gone, Day Is Still Coming, stories and poems by American Indian teenagers and young adults.* He has a beautiful wife, Billie, and two beautiful children, Jordan and Angel.

Jane Yolen has written poetry for young children, older children, and adults. Her poetry books include rhymed picture books like *How Do Dinosaurs Say Goodnight;* unrhymed poem picture books like *Owl Moon;* collections of poetry like *Three Bears Rhyme Book, Color Me a Rhyme, Dear Mother/Dear Daughter, The Radiation Sonnets;* and poetry anthologies like *Once Upon Ice, Weather Report, Alphabestiary,* and *Street Rhymes Around the World.*

GLOSSARY

alliteration

When poets use words that start with the same consonant sound, it is called alliteration. The consonant sounds in alliteration are usually beginning consonant sounds but sometimes they fall in the middle of a word.

> The thin yellow shells crunch
> and crackle as I
> run along the sand.

assonance

Assonance occurs when words share the same vowel sound but the ending consonants are different.

> My coat was quickly covered
> with snowflakes
> when I opened the door
> in the overpowering wind.

beat

Also called *stress*.

The beat in poetry is similar to the beat in music.

When there are three beats in a line it is called *tetrameter*. The line below is in *iambic tetrameter*. *Iambic* means the line of poetry is divided into pairs of syllables with one unstressed syllable followed by one stressed syllable (da DA).

The long lines below show which syllables are stressed.

> da   DA da DA da DA
> ˘   /   ˘ / ˘   /
> My feet are really sore.

The line below has four beats. It is in *iambic quatrameter*.

> da DA da DA da DA da DA
> ˘   /   ˘ / ˘ / ˘ /
> My feet are really sore today.

The next line has five beats. It is in *iambic pentameter*, which most resembles the sound of normal speech.

da DA da DA da DA da DA da DA
ˇ / ˇ / ˇ / ˇ / ˇ /
My tender feet are really sore today.

cadence

rhythm or beat

consonance

Consonance occurs when words share an ending consonant sound but their vowels are different. This often creates a *slant rhyme*. (See *slant rhyme*.)

> live   leave
>
> crib   nab
>
> give   move

couplet

When a poem is divided into two-line stanzas, each pair of lines is called a *couplet*. Couplets usually rhyme.

enjambment, run-ons

Sometimes poets do not break a line or a stanza at a natural place. They "force" the reader to go on to the next line to finish the thought or phrase.

> Home is where you
> can shrug off your
> backpack and your
>
> worries, sling around
> your complaints about
> impossible questions on the science
> test, and supposedly best . . .

image

Poets paint pictures that you can see in your mind's eye. They paint the pictures or images with words. Often the use of metaphor, simile or personification can paint a vivid picture.

internal rhyme

Rhyming words don't have to be located at the ends of lines. Sometimes words in the middle of lines can rhyme and create an interesting effect. For internal rhyme, rhyming words can be sprinkled anywhere in the poem, even next to each other, as long as words that rhyme aren't at the ends of lines.

> The <u>crows</u> are caw cawing.
> The <u>snow</u> came early
> and they're late to <u>go</u>
> south.

line break

The lines in poems are generally shorter than in prose. The poet thinks carefully about where to break each line. Where the line is broken can change the meaning or the feel of a poem.

Sometimes the break comes at a natural pause, such as at the end of a phrase or thought, or where the reader or poet naturally takes a breath.

Sometimes a line break comes in an "unnatural" place, which makes the reader move on to the next line to complete the thought or phrase. This is called *enjambment*, or *run ons*.

This stanza breaks at natural pauses:

> I plunged headfirst
> into the icy water
> before I could change my mind.

This stanza breaks at unnatural places:

> I plunged headfirst into
> the icy water before I
> could change my
> mind.

Sometimes poets break lines according to the number of syllables they want per line.

Often poets play around with unusual line breaks to startle you.

> I went fly
> ing off the
> edge
> of
> the
> cliff.

lyrical

If a poem has traditionally beautiful, musical language, it is called lyrical. Lyric is also used to describe a poem that is subjective, or personal, and uses the pronoun *I*.

metaphor

Poets often use comparisons in poems, in which they use the qualities of one thing to describe another. If the two things are dissimilar, it is called a metaphor.

> My jealousy is an open scab.
> My grandfather's grizzly-bear snarl.

meter

Meter refers to the rhythmic beat of the poem. Because many poets think about rhythm, they pay attention to how words and groups of words are pronounced. They notice which syllables are stressed—where the beat falls. For example, the words beLIEVE and TOtal are pronounced differently. In one, the stress is on the second syllable and in the other on the first syllable.

Poets made up names for groups of syllables, depending on where the stress falls.

Names of Different Units of Meter	Sample Words
da DA is called an *iamb*	confuse, believe
DA da is called a *trochee*	total, rodent, nephew
DA da da is called a *dactyl*	multiply, fanciful, chickadee
da da DA is called an *anapest*	tambourine, Tweedledee, Halloween
DA Da is called a *spondee*	Go home!

When you have a whole line of poetry, in iambs, for example, the stresses don't neatly match up with words as they do above. They match up with syllables.

˘ / ˘ / ˘ / ˘ / ˘ /
Amelia is my friend forevermore.

(See *rhythm*.)

onomatopoeia

When words sound like what they mean, it is called onomatopoeia. *Chirp, slop, slash, dart,* and *crush* are examples of onomatopoeia.

open mic

At a poetry reading called an open mic, poets take turns reading their poetry to an audience. In the classroom, the teacher or a student could act as an emcee and announce each person, by giving the poet's name, the name of the poem, and any other information, such as the person's style of writing.

personification

When a poet uses personification, he or she gives human qualities to an object, a place, an animal or an abstract idea. The poet can make the inanimate entity speak, give it human characteristics, or speak to it as if it were human.

quatrain

A quatrain is a four line stanza.

rhyme scheme

A rhyme scheme is the pattern in which words rhyme in a poem. To denote a rhyme scheme, poets often use letters such as ABAB.

The tree is bare.	A
It has no leaves.	B
It doesn't care,	A
though there's a breeze.	B

The first and third lines rhyme and the second and fourth lines rhyme.

rhythm

The rhythm of a poem is called the *meter* of the poem. When you clap out the poem, where do you clap?

A variety of meters are used by poets. (See *meter.*) Poets can use a particular meter throughout a line of a poem or throughout the whole poem. They can also vary the meter or use combinations of meters.

Below are lines written in particular meters. The long lines show which syllables are stressed.

This line is written in iambs (da DA)

˘ / ˘ / ˘ / ˘ / ˘ /

I seem to be so nasty when I'm tired.

This line is written in trochees. (DA da)

/ ˘ / ˘ / ˘ /

Don't go out if you're unwell!

This line is written in dactyls. (Da da da)

/ ˘ ˘ / ˘ ˘ / ˘ ˘ /

Visit the goblins in Mulberry Dune.

This line is written in anapests. (da da DA)

˘ ˘ / ˘ ˘ / ˘ ˘ / ˘ ˘ /

By the oak near the shore rests a small crimson boat.

This line is written in spondees. (DA DA)

/ / / / / / / /

Be still, don't cry, bad ghouls are here!

simile

Poets often use comparisons in poems, in which they use the qualities of one thing to describe another. If the two things are dissimilar and the comparison uses qualifying words such as *like* or *as*, it is called a *simile.*

His hands looked like brown shriveled leaves at the end of autumn.

slant rhyme

Also called *off-rhyme, part rhyme,* or *near rhyme.*

Some words rhyme perfectly. Other words that sound like they almost rhyme are called slant rhymes. Often the words have consonance. (See *consonance.*)

know and snow are perfect rhymes.
lawn and lone are slant rhymes.
move and love are also slant rhymes.

spacing (See *white space*.)

stanza

Poems are divided into verses that are also called stanzas. There is a space between stanzas. A stanza is like a paragraph in prose.

syllabication

Syllables are important in poetry. Poets have names for groups of syllables, in accordance with the number of syllables and the pattern of the stresses. (See *meter*.)

Syllables can also be important for breaking a line. Some poets count syllables to make sure there are the same number of syllables in each line. Or they write the poem so that there is a pattern, such as 6 syllables in the first line of each stanza, 3 in the second line, and 2 in the last line.

Some poets play with syllables by breaking a word in the middle.

> The fo-
> rest
> is
> soothing.

tone

The tone of the poem relates to the voice of the poet or narrator of the poem. It gives a hint as to the attitude or mood of the poem. Some examples of tone include sarcastic, serious, gentle, instructional, menacing, soothing, joking, and lighthearted.

triolet

The triolet is an 8-line poetry form in which the first line is repeated three times and the second line is repeated in the eighth line.

verse

Verse is an informal word for *stanza*.

white space

White space is an issue with most poems because the lines are broken, and more white space appears on the page than with other forms of writing. Poems can be left-justified, right-justified, or centered. The words can be scattered all over the page or arranged in any creative formation.

Poets also play with white space, sometimes using it visually:

> wh te
> sn wflakes
> f lling

Indents, which create white space, can also mimic the meaning of the text:

> The girls threw the ball
> back   and forth.

Indentations can be used effectively to highlight a part of the poem:

My thoughts
    raced
    dashed
    spun
inside my head.

INDEX